SELF-LEARNING MANAGEMENT SERIES

**VIBRANT**
PUBLISHERS

# SALES MANAGEMENT ESSENTIALS

## YOU ALWAYS WANTED TO KNOW

Ready reckoner on Sales management fundamentals and their practical applications

## VISHAL DESAI

Edited by **Dr. James Ashton**

# Sales Management Essentials You Always Wanted To Know

**First Edition**

© 2022, By Vibrant Publishers, USA. All rights reserved. No part of this publication may be reproduced or distributed in any form or by any means, or stored in a database or retrieval system, without the prior permission of the publisher.

Paperback ISBN 10: 1-63651-074-4
Paperback ISBN 13: 978-1-63651-074-3

Ebook ISBN 10: 1-63651-075-2
Ebook ISBN 13: 978-1-63651-075-0

Hardback ISBN 10: 1-63651-076-0
Hardback ISBN 13: 978-1-63651-076-7

Library of Congress Control Number: 2021947361

Vibrant Publishers books are available at special quantity discount for sales promotions, or for use in corporate training programs. For more information please write to bulkorders@vibrantpublishers.com

Please email feedback / corrections (technical, grammatical or spelling) to spellerrors@vibrantpublishers.com

To access the complete catalogue of Vibrant Publishers, visit www.vibrantpublishers.com

## SELF-LEARNING MANAGEMENT SERIES

| TITLE | PAPERBACK* ISBN |
|---|---|

### ACCOUNTING, FINANCE & ECONOMICS

| | |
|---|---|
| COST ACCOUNTING AND MANAGEMENT ESSENTIALS | 9781636511030 |
| FINANCIAL ACCOUNTING ESSENTIALS | 9781636510972 |
| FINANCIAL MANAGEMENT ESSENTIALS | 9781636511009 |
| MACROECONOMICS ESSENTIALS | 9781636511818 |
| MICROECONOMICS ESSENTIALS | 9781636511153 |
| PERSONAL FINANCE ESSENTIALS | 9781636511849 |

### ENTREPRENEURSHIP & STRATEGY

| | |
|---|---|
| BUSINESS PLAN ESSENTIALS | 9781636511214 |
| BUSINESS STRATEGY ESSENTIALS | 9781949395778 |
| ENTREPRENEURSHIP ESSENTIALS | 9781636511603 |

### GENERAL MANAGEMENT

| | |
|---|---|
| BUSINESS LAW ESSENTIALS | 9781636511702 |
| DECISION MAKING ESSENTIALS | 9781636510026 |
| LEADERSHIP ESSENTIALS | 9781636510316 |
| PRINCIPLES OF MANAGEMENT ESSENTIALS | 9781636511542 |
| TIME MANAGEMENT ESSENTIALS | 9781636511665 |

*Also available in Hardback & Ebook formats

# SELF-LEARNING MANAGEMENT SERIES

| TITLE | PAPERBACK* ISBN |
|---|---|

## HUMAN RESOURCE MANAGEMENT

| TITLE | PAPERBACK* ISBN |
|---|---|
| DIVERSITY IN THE WORKPLACE ESSENTIALS | 9781636511122 |
| HR ANALYTICS ESSENTIALS | 9781636510347 |
| HUMAN RESOURCE MANAGEMENT ESSENTIALS | 9781949395839 |
| ORGANIZATIONAL BEHAVIOR ESSENTIALS | 9781636510378 |
| ORGANIZATIONAL DEVELOPMENT ESSENTIALS | 9781636511481 |

## MARKETING & SALES MANAGEMENT

| TITLE | PAPERBACK* ISBN |
|---|---|
| DIGITAL MARKETING ESSENTIALS | 9781949395747 |
| MARKETING MANAGEMENT ESSENTIALS | 9781636511788 |
| SALES MANAGEMENT ESSENTIALS | 9781636510743 |
| SERVICES MARKETING ESSENTIALS | 9781636511733 |

## OPERATIONS & PROJECT MANAGEMENT

| TITLE | PAPERBACK* ISBN |
|---|---|
| AGILE ESSENTIALS | 9781636510057 |
| OPERATIONS & SUPPLY CHAIN MANAGEMENT ESSENTIALS | 9781949395242 |
| PROJECT MANAGEMENT ESSENTIALS | 9781636510712 |
| STAKEHOLDER ENGAGEMENT ESSENTIALS | 9781636511511 |

*Also available in Hardback & Ebook formats

# About the Author

Vishal has two decades of formidable work experience as Category and Business Head at leading Indian movies and gaming entertainment companies viz: Reliance ADAG's Zapak.com, Shemaroo Entertainment Limited, and Milestone Interactive Group. He has worked extensively in sales and marketing strategy, brand and product management, and corporate strategy. His expertise lies in launching new products with the right marketing mix strategy and managing products through their entire life cycle. His portfolio of brandsn launched while working at Indian licensee companies includes Sony PlayStation One, Slumdog Millionaire, Spiderman, WWE Raw, and several other entertainment franchises across gaming and movie entertainment. He has been a speaker and delegate at various conferences and seminars and has written articles in leading print publications. He is passionate about quizzing and management strategy games and has won the International Business Simulation competition organized by Virginia Commonwealth University. He also regularly organizes business quiz competitions for students at Indian B-Schools. As a subject matter expert, he has contributed towards the development of educational e-content for Govt. Of India's University Grants Commission. He teaches at media and management institutes as a visiting faculty member. He is a management graduate from NMIMS University, India.

## Other contributors

We would like to thank our editor, **Dr. James Ashton,** for his contribution to making this book the best version possible. Dr. James Ashton is a dedicated higher education professional with more than 20 years of direct classroom (online and on-campus) experience showing commitment to excellence in teaching. He is a multilingual educator interested in improving the learning process and adapting methods and styles to the individual needs of every student.

# What experts say about this book!

Vishal Desai provides a digestible introduction to complex sales and management concepts. The topics in this book will give anyone, at any level, a succinct overview of these sales and management essentials along with helpful visual guides that can be used for teams or for professional development.

> **– Michelle Bartonico,**
> **Trinity University**

This exciting book is a perfect teaching tool for sales management courses or corporate training programs. Business professors, instructors, sales managers, salesforce personnel, and students will enjoy reading these exciting materials.

> **– Thomas Li-Ping Tang, Ph.D.,**
> **Professor of Management,**
> **Jennings A. Jones College of Business**

The lucidity with which the book is written shows an industry experience perspective of the third eye on the Sales Management Cycle.

> **– Dr. C.N.Narayana,**
> **Former Senior Professor & DG,**
> **Kirloskar Institute and IIEBM**

# What experts say about this book!

Vishal Desai's straightforward style lends itself to insights and pronouncements about how sales management and marketing should be understood as the drivers of the success of any organization. The cases and class assignments are a special bonus for professors to use to help reinforce learning.

> – **Joseph Stasio,**
> **Associate Professor of Marketing,**
> **Merrimack College**

This book succinctly is a step-by-step easy-to-implement learner's guide to understand sales in the dynamic context of business. The best thing about this book is its lucid language, conceptual clarity, and seamless flow.

> – **Prof Ujjwal K Chowdhury,**
> **Strategic Advisor & Professor,**
> **Daffodil International University**

This is an amazing book for students, professors, and sales professionals. It covers fundamental topics in a well-organized manner, including cross-selling vs. up-selling, SKU, push vs. pull strategy, sales channel strategies, and sales management in a post-pandemic era. This book is an excellent guide for learning about sales.

> – **Dr. Eunyoung Jang,**
> **Assistant Professor of Marketing,**
> **Midwestern State University**

# What experts say about this book!

The content matches the title very well--As a sales management "essential," the book is written in a very concise manner. I like that the book embeds marketing channels in the discussion of sales management. An interesting detail is that the book has a separate chapter on the post-pandemic situation of sales.

**– Dr. Jia Li,**
**Associate Professor of Marketing,**
**Wake Forest University**

*This page is intentionally left blank*

# Table of Contents

I wish to express my gratitude to **Vibrant Publishers** for giving me an opportunity to pen this book. Special thanks to my wife Kajal, son Vansh and well-wishers for encouraging me to start my journey as an author.

**– Vishal Desai**

*This page is intentionally left blank*

# Preface

Sales and Marketing as organizational functions are often referred to interchangeably. However, marketing is all about identifying and creating value for the consumers, whereas sales is essentially about delivering value to the consumers in return for a price. At the same time, sales management involves many sub-activities, making it a specialized function within an organization that holds as much importance as marketing.

'Sales Management Essentials You Always Wanted to Know' is a book that explains all the facets of sales in a detailed and lucid manner. It is a ready reckoner that spares one the effort of reading through a traditional and voluminous textbook. It has been specially designed and written for young executives, graduate students, and entrepreneurs who wish to enhance their understanding and knowledge of sales management. The book will also help the teaching fraternity and industry professionals who teach sales and marketing management courses at B-schools. The book contains relevant examples, cases, quizzes, and class assignments, thus enhancing the teaching experience.

*This page is intentionally left blank*

# Introduction to the book

Sales function acts as the bridge between an organization and the final consumers it intends to serve through its market offering. Sales is where most of the action in a business lies because it is a crucial revenue-generating function. Sales management is critical to meet the challenges of increasing competition levels in the marketplace. Effective sales management helps an organization optimize results from its sales channel management and sales force management and achieve the organization's sales objectives. It is thus imperative for one to be familiar with various aspects of sales management.

This book deals with all the essentials of sales management, which are required to make decisions about sales channels, selling techniques, distribution strategy, sales promotion tools, and sales force management to achieve the desired sales objectives.

**By the end of the book, you will be able to:**

- Get a complete understanding of the concepts and approaches required for effective decision-making in sales management

- Implement various sales strategies to maximize sales revenue in today's competitive marketplace

- Understand how to select, manage and evaluate the sales channel members

- Appreciate the importance of sales force management and managing the sales force effectively

- Learn various sales promotion tools to increase the sales revenue of the organization

- Understand how to handle conflict situations in sales management

*This page is intentionally left blank*

# Who can benefit from the book?

- Faculty members, professors, and students of marketing/ business/sales management courses

- Entrepreneurs who wish to enhance their knowledge about sales management practices for the growth of their business

- Working professionals like sales managers and marketing managers who may wish to learn about sales management concepts that they can practice during their career

# How to use this book?

This book can be used as a ready reckoner or a handy guide on Sales and Distribution Management.

- It is suggested to read the chapters in chronological order.

- Readers should use the case studies, case discussions, class assignments which are given at the end of each chapter to reinforce the concepts mentioned in the book

- PowerPoint presentations made available with the book can be used as teaching aids during the class

*This page is intentionally left blank*

# Chapter **1**

# Introduction to Sales Management

This chapter familiarizes the reader with sales management and the set of activities that form a part of this function. The chapter provides an overview of the relative importance of sales functions in an organization and establishes the specialized role of the sales team in achieving the revenue generation goals of an organization. The chapter states the definitions of selling, marketing, and sales management. It outlines the importance of sales as a provider of utility to the consumers and explains how sales management delivers the value created by the marketing process to the customers. It also makes note of the difference between selling and marketing functions within an organization.

Key learning objectives of this chapter include the reader's understanding of the following:

- The nature and concerns of sales management in an organization

- How sales management adds value for both the consumers and the organization

- The difference between sales and marketing functions in terms of their focus areas

- How sales management generates utility for the consumers

# 1.1 Definition of Sale and Sales Management

A 'Sale' can be explained as a transaction that involves the transfer of possession and ownership of tangible goods from the seller to the buyer and /or performance of a particular set of activities or services by the seller for the benefit of the buyer in return for a consideration from the buyer. As per Investopedia. com, 'A sale is a transaction between two or more parties in which the buyer receives tangible or intangible goods, services, or assets in exchange for money or other assets are paid to a seller.'[1]

Sales management, on the other hand, is defined as planning and executing all tasks concerned with selling, selling techniques, sales force management, and distribution of goods and services.

According to the Marketing Accountability Standards Board (MASB), Sales Management is defined as: "The planning, direction, and control of professional selling including recruiting, selecting, equipping, assigning, routing, supervising, paying and motivating as these tasks apply to the sales force."[2]

---

1. https://www.investopedia.com/terms/s/sale.asp

2. *The Common Language Marketing Dictionary*, MASB, ©2020, https://marketing-dictionary.org/s/sales-management/

Sales is the only function in an organization that directly generates revenue or income for a company and hence it needs to be adequately managed. The financial results of a company depend upon the performance of the sales department. Sales operations of an organization depend on the sales strategy adopted by the organization. Optimal sales management is achieved when the sales analysis or desired sales results are aligned with the sales strategy and sales operations (see Figure 1.1).

**Figure 1.1**    **Optimal Sales Management**

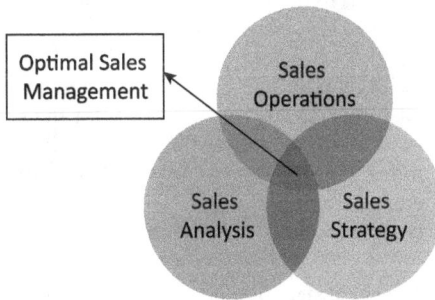

**Source:** *The Investors Book*, Prachi M, July 27, 2019, https://theinvestorsbook.com/sales-management.html

# 1.2 Selling v/s Marketing

Selling and Marketing are so closely interwoven with each other that one can often not identify the differences between both functions. In fact, in lean organizations, the same team typically performs both sales and marketing tasks. Marketing and Selling are both aimed at increasing revenue. However, marketing is different from selling, and as an organization grows, the roles and responsibilities of sales and marketing teams become more specialized. The differences between marketing and sales functions are outlined in Table 1.1.

**Table 1.1**    **Differences between Marketing and Selling**

|  | Marketing | Selling |
|---|---|---|
| **Focus** | • identifying needs of the consumers<br>• finding a solution to meet those needs<br>• communicating the solution to them<br>• offering the solution to them | • delivering the solution to the consumers in the most effective manner |
| **Objective** | • build long term customer loyalty<br>• customer relationship management<br>• ensure lifetime customer value | • match market demand for the solution<br>• maximize sales revenue |
| **Scope of activities** | • market and competition analysis<br>• pricing strategies<br>• integrated marketing communication<br>• managing product life cycle<br>• brand management<br>• capturing the mindshare of the consumer | • manage sales & distribution channels<br>• penetrate existing markets and develop new markets<br>• sales force management<br>• increase market share<br>• demand forecasting |
| **Horizon** | Long term, with the objective of capturing customer lifetime value | Short to medium term to match supply with demand and achieve sales targets |
| **Identity** | Construction of a brand identity that gets associated with a particular need fulfillment | Meeting demand in an opportunistic manner driven by human interaction |

Thus, the goal of marketing is to generate interest and demand for a product through the following activities:

- **Market research** to identify the needs of the customers

- **Product development** to design solutions to meet those needs

- **Advertising** the solutions to create awareness and build the brand

- **Capturing** customer lifetime value to maximize long-term revenue

On the other hand, selling involves directly interacting with the prospects or customers to persuade them to purchase the product. Hence, sales activities are directed towards converting market demand into sales revenue and increasing market share. The set of activities that constitutes sales management are as follows:

- **Appointing** sales channel partners to extend the company's reach for its products and deciding their trade margins, target incentives, etc., while monitoring their performance

- **Developing** new markets and increasing penetration for products in existing markets

- **Managing** the sales force, which includes recruitment, training, monitoring, and evaluating its performance

- **Implementing** trade promotional activities to incentivize the trade intermediaries to buy the company's products

- **Protecting** existing market share from the competitors and further increasing the market share

Marketing, thus, tends to focus on the general population (or a large set of people), whereas selling tends to focus on individuals or a group of prospects.

The selling concept focuses on moving the existing products that an organization produces from their source of origin to the end consumers. The end objective of the selling concept is to generate maximum profits by selling large volumes of the products manufactured by the organization.

The marketing concept, on the other hand, focuses more on identifying consumers' needs and generating profits by satisfying those needs. The differences between both concepts are explained in Figure 1.2.

| Figure 1.2 | **Selling Concept v/s Marketing Concept** |

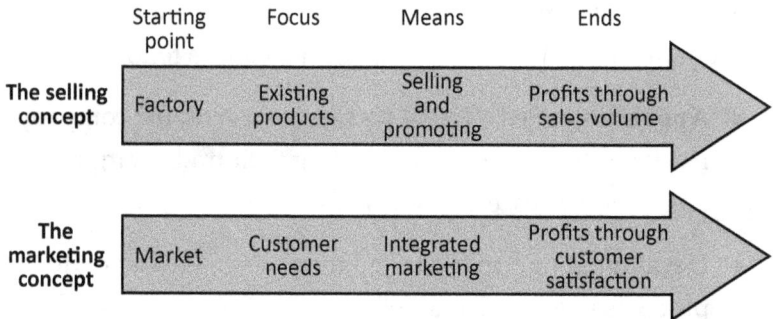

| | Starting point | Focus | Means | Ends |
|---|---|---|---|---|
| **The selling concept** | Factory | Existing products | Selling and promoting | Profits through sales volume |
| **The marketing concept** | Market | Customer needs | Integrated marketing | Profits through customer satisfaction |

Source: https://qsstudy.com/business-studies/contrast-between-selling-concept-and-marketing-concept

# 1.3 Sales Management – Delivering Utility Value

Another way to look at Sales Management is that it delivers utility value to the consumers. Utility refers to the usefulness that consumers experience from a product. It is imperative to understand that consumers seek a set of utilities from the products and services they buy. Thus, selling should necessarily involve adding value to a product by providing the following utilities to the consumers (see Figure 1.3).

**Economic utilities sought by a consumer**

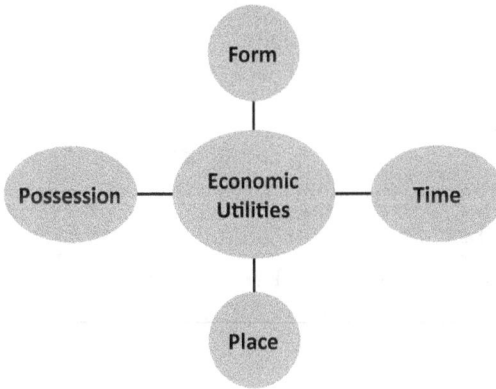

## 1.3.1 Form Utility

Consumers generally look for products in a ready-to-consume state to avoid spending further efforts, time, and money to consume the products. Form utility involves the transformation of raw materials into finished goods. Companies process raw material components, chemicals, or elements to develop a finished product offered to the consumer to meet their specific needs. Many attributes define the form utility of a product. Some of these attributes are shape, size, weight, packaging, and technical specifications. Consumers evaluate the form utility of the products they plan to buy. The higher the form utility of the product, the higher is the price a person may be ready to pay for the product.

**Example:**

i. A consumer who is out to buy a personal desktop computer will have two buying options. One is to buy a ready-to-use computer or buy a kit containing different computer parts and then assemble them to make the computer. The consumer is most likely to pay a higher price for the former offering as it has more form utility than the latter.

## 1.3.2 Time Utility

Time utility is created when a company makes it possible for consumers to buy a product or get it delivered at times that are more convenient or preferred. Time utility also involves deciding the hours and days of the week a company might choose to make its services available. Online purchasing is the most relevant example in which consumers choose the most favorable time slot for receiving or collecting the goods purchased by them. Another example is a pharmacy or a duty-free shop at an airport that is open 24 hours a day to cater to the passengers who may arrive or depart at any time of the day. Time utility might also include 24-hour customer service support through a toll-free phone number or a website chat function. Companies analyze how to maximize their products' time utility and plan the production process, logistics, warehousing, and delivery arrangements accordingly.

**Examples:**

i. Most e-commerce portals like Amazon.com offer customers a choice of delivery speed and time slots to deliver goods they have ordered. The customers can choose the time slot which is the most convenient for them.

ii. Another example is Hewlett Packard offering an auto-replenishment facility for its ink cartridges every few weeks so that its customers do not run out of ink.

iii. A working couple may seek more time utility to get the product delivered at their convenient time.

## 1.3.3 Place Utility

Place utility refers to making goods or services available or accessible to consumers at a maximum number of places to avoid traveling far to buy the products. Examples of place utility range from having a retail store or an ATM or a car service center in a remote location to how easy it is to find a company's website on the internet. Making a product available at a wide variety of stores and locations increases the place utility for the consumers. The idea is to be present at multiple touchpoints from where the consumer is likely to buy or order a particular product or other products that offer similar benefits.

**Examples:**

i. Samsung sells its products not only from its galleries but also through other retail stores and online shopping portals.

ii. Sony PlayStation or Microsoft Xbox are available at stores selling consoles and PC games and at toy stores, electronics stores, music stores, or stores selling computer accessories and peripherals.

iii. Hot and cold beverages are sold at restaurants, gas stations, movie halls, or through vending machines.

iv. A person living in a remote location may seek more place utility so that he/she does not have to travel far to buy a product.

## 1.3.4 Possession Utility

Possession utility signifies the perceived usefulness of a product, which increases by having the right to own and use it freely. For example, owning a car may offer higher possession utility to a person as compared to that offered by a rented car. The reason is that owning a car gives the user the flexibility to use it as per one's choice, a sense of pride for possessing the car, and a resale value for the car.

**Examples:**

i. Companies that sell white goods, consumer durables, furniture or apartments increase the possession utility for the products they sell by offering installment facilities to the consumers who do not have to pay the entire price of the product upfront.

ii. A furniture rental company transfers the ownership of the rented furniture to its customers after they pay rent for 24 months.

Marketers or intermediaries offer a mix of utilities to the consumers depending upon the category of product or service.

Refer to Figure 1.4 to understand form and possession utility.

| Figure 1.4 | Differentiating goods and services retailing using form and possession utilities |
|---|---|

**High**

| | | |
|---|---|---|
| | *Supermarket*<br>*Music & Video store* | *Tailor*<br>*Photo Studio* |
| **Possession<br>Utility** | *Video Rental Library*<br>*Book Library*<br>*Car Rental* | *Hotel*<br>*Airlines*<br>*Night Club*<br>*Theater* |

**Low**                                                    **High**

**Form Utility**

Source: Winsor, Robert & Sheth, Jagdish & Manolis, Chris. (2004). *Journal of Business Research*, Elsevier, vol. 57(3), pages 249-255, March

## 1.3.5 High Possession Utility and Low Form Utility

Here the intermediaries offer high possession utility and low form utility because the form of the products is already well defined by the marketer, whereas the intermediaries predominantly transfer the possession of the products to the consumers.

**Example:**

i.  A supermarket does not change the form of the physical products that it sells and essentially transfers the possession of those products to the consumers for a price.

## 1.3.6 High Possession Utility and High Form Utility

Some marketers or intermediaries process raw materials provided by their customers to make a finished product by changing the form of the inputs. This product is customized as per the specifications provided by each customer. The possession of this finished product is then transferred to the customer after receiving the service charges. In this case the customer is getting high form utility as well as possession utility.

**Example:**

i.  Tailoring service providers convert raw materials like cloth, buttons, and a zipper into a garment which possesses a higher form utility than the individual raw materials. The customer is then charged a service fee for the services rendered and for the transfer of possession and ownership of the final product.

## 1.3.7 Low Possession Utility and High Form Utility

Here the marketers or intermediaries offer high form utility but low possession utility. The product offering is such that a mix of physical goods and services is used to generate high form utility in real-time at the point of consumption, but the consumers do not gain possession utility of the final offering.

**Examples:**

i.  A hotel offers the physical form of its hotel room and furnishings to offer output in another form, i.e., rest, accommodation, and sleep for the customers. However, the customers cannot take possession and ownership of the hotel room.

ii. A restaurant that offers a dine-in facility converts the food ingredients into a meal that is consumed using complementary physical amenities like the dining table, chair, and tableware, as well as by availing complementary services of a cook and a waiter. However, the customers cannot gain the possession utility of the physical amenities as they have not bought the same.

## 1.3.8 Low Possession Utility and Low Form Utility

In the case of certain physical products, the form of the offering cannot be changed at the point of sale or consumption. Also, the consumers get only temporary possession of the product without gaining any ownership benefits. Thus both possession and form utilities offered to the consumers are low.

**Example:**

i. Video or book circulating libraries give temporary possession of DVDs or books to their members by renting out the same to them. The members have to transfer the possession of the DVDs or books back to the libraries after using the same for a certain period.

In this case, the form of the product does not change at the point of sale, nor does the consumer retain possession of the product. The ownership of the product also remains with the marketer or the intermediary.

Before making the purchase decision, a consumer evaluates the total perceived quantum of utility that they will get from the product or service being offered by the company. This quantum will be different for each consumer depending on the mix of utilities, i.e., form, place, time, and possession, being sought by each consumer.

## 1.3.9 To summarize:

- Form Utility is about offering products in a **ready-to-consume state.**

- Possession Utility is about transferring the **possession and ownership** of products to the consumers.

- Time Utility is about making products **readily available** at most times.

- Place Utility is about taking products **closer** to the consumer from places of production.

# Chapter Summary

◆ Sales management essentially delivers value to the consumers by providing time, place, form, and possession utilities.

◆ Sales management is a specialized function with a clear set of defined objectives and techniques to increase sales revenue within an organization.

◆ Selling holds a weightage similar to that of marketing in an organization.

◆ Sales and marketing teams in an organization have to work in sync to meet the challenges of the marketplace and also to gain from the opportunities available in the dynamic business environment.

In the subsequent chapters, we shall explore each sales function, selling technique, and sales strategy which are the core essentials of sales management.

# Quiz 1

1. **Form utility is about:**

   a. Offering products in a ready-to-consume state

   b. Transferring ownership of the products

   c. Making products readily available at most of the times

   d. Taking products closer to the consumer from places of production

2. **Time utility is about:**

   a. Offering products in a ready-to-consume state

   b. Transferring ownership of the products

   c. Making products readily available at most of the times

   d. Taking products closer to the consumer from places of production

3. **Place utility is about:**

   a. Offering products in a ready to consume state

   b. Transferring ownership of the products

   c. Making products readily available at most times

   d. Taking products closer to the consumer from the places of production

4. **Possession utility is about:**

   a. Offering products in a ready-to-consume state

   b. Transferring ownership of the products

   c. Making products readily available at most times

   d. Taking products closer to the consumer from the places of production

5. **Sales is about:**

   a. Finding a solution to consumer's needs

   b. Creating value for the organization

   c. Delivering value to the consumers

   d. None of the above

6. **Marketing is about:**

   a. Construction of a brand identity which gets associated with a particular need

   b. Establishing and managing distribution channels

   c. Meeting demand in an opportunistic manner driven by human interaction

   d. Ability to meet demand at the right time

**7. Offering installment payment facility to the consumer creates:**

   a. Time utility

   b. Possession utility

   c. Place utility

   d. All of the above

**8. Sales management includes:**

   a. Sales force management

   b. Delivering value to the consumers

   c. Distribution of products or services

   d. All of the above

**9. Which form of utility is created when a multiplex cinema offers an online seat booking facility?**

   a. Time

   b. Place

   c. Possession

   d. Options A & B

10. **Which of the following comes under the scope of sales management?**

   a. To penetrate new markets

   b. To ensure repeat purchases by customers

   c. To undertake demand forecasting

   d. All of the above

| **Answers** | 1 – a | 2 – c | 3 – d | 4 – b | 5 – c |
|-------------|-------|-------|-------|-------|-------|
|             | 6 – a | 7 – b | 8 – d | 9 – b | 10 – d |

# Class Activity

The class can be given a mix of ten products. Each student can be told to rank the most important and the least essential utility that he or she seeks while purchasing each of these products. The most important utility can be given a score of four, and the least essential utility a score of one. Then calculate the average score of each utility for each of the products for the entire class. The utility with the highest score for each product is the most sought after by the consumers for the respective product. This average score can be considered indicative of the consumers' expectations at large.

# Chapter **2**

# Sales Channels and Process

This chapter gives an overview of the sales channels adopted by companies to ensure that their products are distributed most effectively. Products or services are sold through varied distribution channels depending on their category and the end consumer. Moreover, one must understand how, when and where consumers prefer to buy various products or services. Since different consumers have different buying preferences, companies may use multiple sales channels to reach the maximum number of consumers.

Key learning objectives of this chapter include the reader's understanding of the following:

- Types of sales channels used by companies depending upon the nature of products and services

- The factors to be considered for selecting the ideal sales channel

- The chain of channel partners to be followed for distribution of products.

Sales channels can be broadly classified as follows:

a. Business to Consumer (B2C)

b. Direct to Consumer (D2C)

c. Business to Business (B2B)

d. Business to Government (B2G)

e. Omni-Channel Distribution

## 2.1 Business to Consumer (B2C) Channel

In order to serve a broad base of consumers, companies in general distribute their products through a chain of intermediaries or channel partners. Such a sales channel is called the Business to Consumer (B2C) sales channel, leading to individual end consumers who buy and consume the products for their personal use. The channel consists of distributors, wholesalers, retailers, direct selling agents, online shopping portals who make the products readily available to the customers on demand. Here the distributor is an entity that buys a marketer's products in bulk and then breaks the bulk into smaller lots to further sell them to wholesalers, retail stores, or online shopping portals that cater to the end consumers. These intermediaries get a certain trade margin on the retail or street price. The amount of such trade margin for the intermediaries is largely pre-defined by the marketer. The company may choose to appoint a different set of intermediaries for different markets. These intermediaries can be appointed either on an exclusive basis or a non-exclusive basis. At the same time, the number of intermediaries that form the chain of distribution can vary depending on various factors. The total number of intermediaries involved in the channel thus form the 'Channel Width' for distributing the products.

B2C sales channels can be further classified into intensive distribution channel, selective distribution channel, exclusive distribution channel, television home shopping, and network marketing (multi-level marketing).

## 2.1.1 Intensive Distribution Channel

Mass consumption products like household & personal care products, convenience goods, grocery, and food products require an intensive distribution chain with several intermediaries to reach the targeted end consumers. Consumers buy or order such products with high frequency or almost daily; hence a company needs to have several touchpoints for consumers to order or buy these products frequently. These could be physical retail stores or online portals.

The typical distribution channel for intensive distribution is illustrated in Figure 2.1.

**Figure 2.1**  **Intensive Distribution Channel**

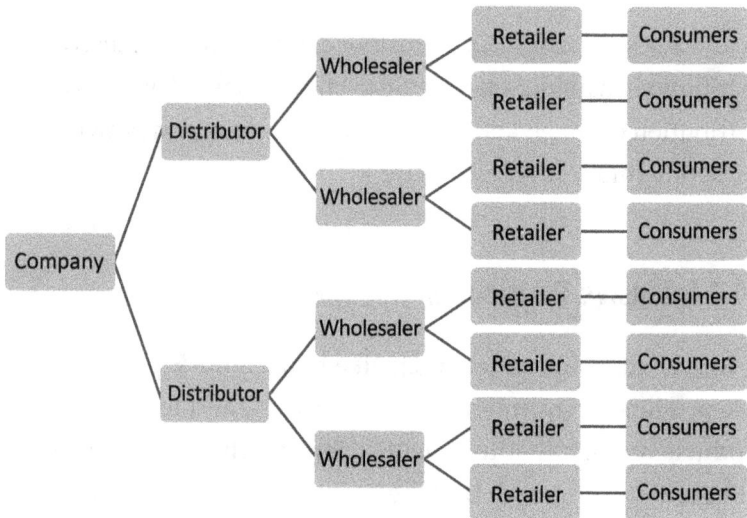

**Note:** Retailers are either offline stores or online shopping portals.

Typically, a distributor is appointed for each primary market or region. The distributor further sells the products to wholesalers who cater to specific clusters within the market and supply them to retailers of these clusters. Retailers further sell the products to end consumers.

## 2.1.2 Selective Distribution Channel

Shopping goods like watches, apparel, consumer durables, gaming consoles, or body perfumes are bought at less frequent intervals than mass products and are sold through a selective distribution channel, as illustrated in Figure 2.2.

**Figure 2.2** **Selective Distribution Channel**

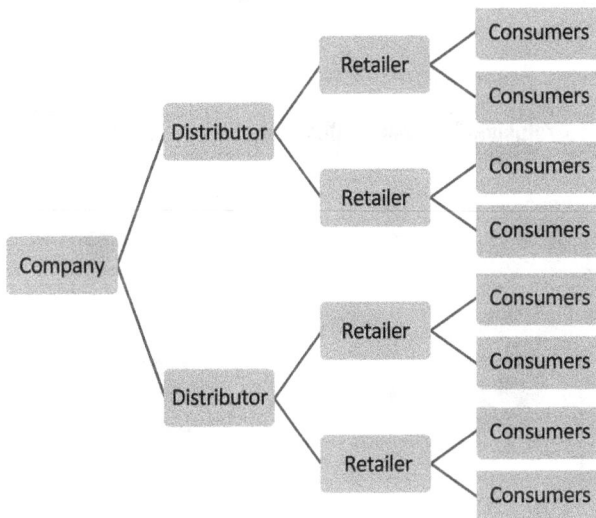

Note: Retailers are either offline stores or online shopping portals.

## 2.1.3 Exclusive Distribution Channel

Products like high-end automobiles, premium watches, precious jewelry, high-end electronics, and holiday packages— all of which are considered luxury goods— are sold through exclusive retail stores or franchise outlets serviced directly by the marketer. These stores exclusively sell products of a particular brand only as per guidelines set by the marketer of that brand. The nature of the above products is such that a vast distribution network is not required because the size of the target audience is comparatively smaller for products that require selective or intensive distribution. Also, the buying frequency for such products is comparatively lower as compared to the buying frequency for mass consumption products. Some companies may also choose to sell their products through 'Company Owned Company Operated' (COCO) stores to ensure good customer service standards. Figure 2.3 illustrates the Exclusive Distribution Channel.

**Figure 2.3**    **Exclusive Distribution Channel**

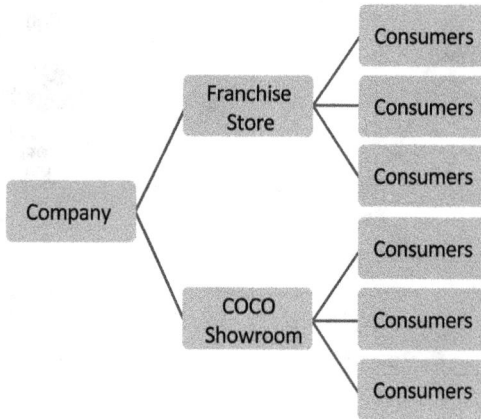

Besides the number of intermediaries involved, each of the above distribution channels have distinct characteristics, as explained in Table 2.1.

| Table 2.1 | Characteristics of Intensive, Selective, and Exclusive Distribution Channels |
|---|---|

|  | Intensive | Selective | Exclusive |
|---|---|---|---|
| **Product categories** | Household & personal care, convenience goods, food products, medicines, over-the-counter drugs, stationery | Watches, spare parts, apparel, books, consumer durables, gaming consoles, perfumes, footwear, sports goods | Luxury watches, automobiles, precious jewelry, holiday packages, timeshare resort memberships |
| **Channel Width** | Large | Medium | Small |
| **Frequency of purchase by the consumer** | Daily/Weekly | Few months/ Years | Extended time frame |
| **Persuasion strategy** | Product sampling and trial packs | Free trial/ Product demonstration | Product trial/ Product demonstration |
| **Salesforce size** | Large | Medium | Small |
| **Territory covered per salesperson** | **Metros:** 4-5 miles radius **Semi urban:** Entire town **Rural:** cluster of villages | **Metros:** 8-10 miles radius **Semi Urban:** Entire town | Entire City/ State/Zone |
| **Inventory replenishment frequency** | Daily / Weekly | Weekly / Fortnightly | Weekly / Forthrightly / Monthly |
| **General distribution arrangement with channel partners** | Non-Exclusive | Exclusive / Non-Exclusive | Exclusive |

|  | Intensive | Selective | Exclusive |
|---|---|---|---|
| **Trade Margin for channel partners** | Low to Medium | Medium to High | Medium to High |
| **Advertising Budgets** | High | Medium to High | Medium to High |

**Note:** The above table is only indicative, and there can be exceptions. A company may choose to skip or add any intermediary in the chain based on the sales strategy adopted by the company.

## 2.1.4 Television Home Shopping

Some companies that specialize in selling innovative and impulse buying products may prefer to sell through television (TV) shopping channels. The channels advertise products demonstrating functionality to the viewers in a 3 to 5 minutes capsule, and a substantial discount on the street price is offered for such products by the marketer. In return, the shopping channels either get a commission on the product sold or may charge the seller for the advertising capsule on their TV channels. Some of the products sold through this channel are body shaping products, health, and well-being products, low-end electronic products, cleaning products, and kitchenware.

## 2.1.5 Network Marketing or Multi-Level Marketing (MLM)

Network Marketing or Multi-Level Marketing is a sales model in which companies appoint independent representatives for selling products within their social circle, by often working from home. Additionally, they may be required to appoint sub-agents who can further sell the products. The strategy is to build a pyramid structure consisting of an independent salesforce for the company. The advantage of this strategy is that companies do not have to spend vast sums of money in advertising their products. Furthermore, there are less intermediaries involved in the chain; thus, companies save on the trade margins otherwise paid to them. Tupperware and Amway, which sell various household and personal care products, are some of the best examples of this type of sales channel. The hierarchy of sales agents in Network Marketing or MLM is as illustrated in Figure 2.4.

**Figure 2.4  Network Marketing or Multi-Level Marketing**

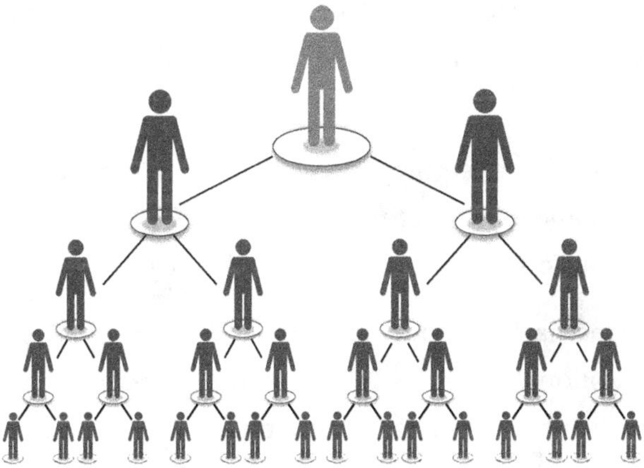

Source: https://magazine.lectera.com/articles/why-and-how-to-study-network-marketing

Some of the advantages of the B2C sales channel are as follows:

a. A company does not have to create its distribution infrastructure to serve the entire market, thus leading to cost savings.

b. Since the intermediaries regularly service the consumers' demand, a company does not have to deploy its resources for day-to-day operational activities, and thus, it can focus on more significant market development efforts and analysis.

c. The company's working capital requirements are comparatively less because the intermediaries invest in inventory and warehousing for their respective territories allotted by the marketer.

d. Once the goods are sold to the intermediaries, the commercial risks associated with unsold products, bad debts, pilferage, product damage, and product expiry are passed on to the intermediaries.

e. The salesforce requirements of the company reduces to quite some extent because the intermediaries also recruit their salesforce to cater to the market needs.

f. Intermediaries help the company implement sales promotional activities by distributing product brochures, leaflets, product samples, trial packs, gifts, etc., to the target audience.

Some of the disadvantages of the B2C sales channel are as follows:

a. At times, a company may have over-dependence on the intermediaries who may try to negotiate those terms of business that are most favorable to them.

b. If the intermediaries run out of inventory or if the chain of distribution breaks at any point, the marketer may lose sales revenue till the inventory is replenished or the chain is re-established.

c. A company may face the following issues with the intermediaries:

- Non-performance as per the company's expectations

- Payment delays or default

- Breach of trade terms

- Conflict concerning business terms and conditions

## 2.2 Direct to Consumer (D2C) Channel

As the name suggests, Direct to Consumer (D2C) Channel means selling directly to the end consumers, thus eliminating the need for intermediaries. Some of the products which are sold through the D2C channel include the following:

a. Innovative products that require a demonstration of the product's functionality and features. For example:

- A newly-introduced electronic machine for cooking

- 3D printers that can print and make artificial body parts

- A robot that can serve food at restaurants

b. Services that require consultative selling like wealth management, career counseling, timeshare resorts, etc.

c. Products or services that require site visits like real estate, banquet services, and club memberships

d. Products sold through mail-order catalogs in remote areas where there are advertising constraints

e. Rental services for furniture, self-drive cars, books,and DVDs

f. Specialty products like health and hygiene products, herbal products, lifestyle and wellbeing products sold exclusively on websites and social media platforms like Facebook and WhatsApp.

Figure 2.5 illustrates the structure of a Direct to Consumer (D2C) Channel, which does not involve any channel intermediaries.

---

**Figure 2.5**   **Direct to Consumer (D2C) Channel**

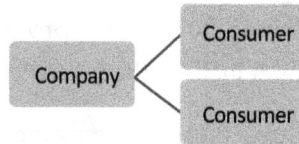

**Examples of products being sold through the D2C channel:**

- Casper brand of bed products

- Away brand of luggage products

- Man Matters brand of men's grooming and wellness products

- Let's Shave brand of shaving products

- The Derma Company brand of products for skin care

Some of the advantages of the D2C sales channel are as follows:

a. Companies get real-time feedback on consumer behavior which can help them further enhance the consumer experience

b. Since no intermediaries are involved in this channel, companies can save money on trade margins or commissions to be paid to the intermediaries, thus increasing their profitability

c. Target consumers can be exposed to an entire range of marketer's products without any dependence on intermediaries

Some of the disadvantages of the D2C sales channel are as follows:

a. The commercial risk of doing business rests solely with the marketer as there are no intermediaries involved

b. All operational tasks involved in catering to the end consumer have to be managed by the marketer. This calls for allocating additional resources and working capital investment by the marketer

c. It may take more time to achieve higher sales volumes than what it takes through B2C channels

Finally, marketers have to evaluate the cost-benefit ratio involved in a D2C channel to decide whether they wish to adopt the same to align with the goals and objectives of the organization.

# 2.3 Business to Business (B2B) Channel

Besides selling to the end consumers, marketers also sell their products in bulk to organizations or institutions for their internal consumption. This is referred to as the Business to Business or B2B sales channel. Marketers generally prefer to deal directly with customers who order products in large quantities at a special price (see Figure 2.6).

---

**Figure 2.6**    **Business to Business (B2B) Channel**

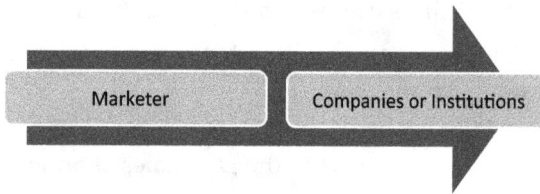

---

Marketer → Companies or Institutions

**Examples:**

a. Mobile phone screen or battery makers sell their products to mobile phone manufacturers

b. Book publishers sell their books to libraries

c. Car wiper blades manufacturers sell their products to car manufacturers

d. Wrist watch strap makers sell their products to watch manufacturers

e. Zip manufacturers sell their products to apparel makers

Marketers that sell key components or equipment used in manufacturing of new products are referred to as **Original Equipment Manufacturers (OEMs).**

For the B2B channel, the sales process involves seven steps as illustrated in Figure 2.7.

**Figure 2.7** **Seven Steps of B2B Sales Channel**

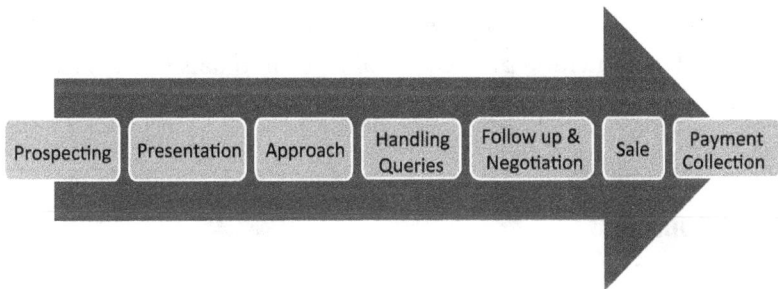

Prospecting | Presentation | Approach | Handling Queries | Follow up & Negotiation | Sale | Payment Collection

## 2.3.1 Prospecting

Prospecting starts with making a database of potential prospects who may need a product or service. This database can be compiled from secondary sources like trade magazines, websites, or industry reports. On the other hand, primary sources include leads generated by the company's marketing efforts like digital advertising, participating in trade and consumer exhibitions, or references from existing and past customers, vendors, friends, and colleagues.

It is imperative to note that it is not enough to find only one prospect at a target company. There could be multiple prospects depending on its organizational structure and roles and responsibilities of internal teams. Hence one will have to practice multi-threading to connect with multiple decision-makers at the prospect organization.

## 2.3.2 Presentation

The next step is to be prepared for the initial contact with a prospect by researching the market and collecting all relevant information regarding a product or service. At this point, one has to develop sales presentations, leaflets, product catalog, and/or audio/video content for the company's products or services. These should ideally include product details, testimonials from existing and past customers, product samples, trial packs etc.

## 2.3.3 Approach

In the approach stage, one has to contact the prospect and request a face-to-face meeting. There are three standard approach methods:

1. **Gifting approach:** Presenting a potential client with a gift at the beginning of an interaction.

   **Example:**

   A pharma company's Medical Representatives (MRs) present a small gift to the doctors, with its brand name printed on it for easy recall.

2. **Question approach:** Asking questions related to the prospect's needs or problem areas and pitching the product or service as an ideal solution.

**Example:**

A prospect wanting to buy computers for his company's employees can be asked questions about the type of work done by the employees, software applications required to be installed in the computers, hard disc capacity required, size of monitor required. This approach helps to crystallize the prospect's exact needs so that a set of products and services can be suggested to fulfill their needs.

3. **Product approach**

This approach is best suited for new products whose functionality needs to be emphasized to convert the prospect into a buyer. The prospect is given either a trial pack of the product or offered a product demonstration to review the product. This is one of the most effective approaches because the product's benefits can be explained to the prospect in an effective and live manner.

**Examples:**

a. When vacuum cleaners were newly introduced, the sales executives demonstrated its superior cleaning abilities compared to that of a traditional broom

b. A company selling beverage vending machines offers to install one for a short trial period at the prospects' location so that they can experience the product features before placing the final order

## 2.3.4 Handling Queries

Once the salesperson completes the presentation and sales pitch, there may be some queries or objections raised by the prospect. Following are some of the areas in which queries can be raised:

i. Customization of the product to suit the prospect's needs

ii. Possibility of printing prospect's brand logo on the product or its packaging

iii. Lead time between ordering the products and delivery to the prospect's warehouse

iv. Payment or credit terms offered to the prospect

v. Approximate price of products or discount offered for bulk quantity purchases

The sales person then sends a quotation for the supply of goods with terms and conditions.

## 2.3.5 Follow-up & Negotiation

Having sent the quotation, the salesperson has to follow up with the prospects to know their feedback. Once the prospect has shortlisted the marketer's products, the sales person will be called for further negotiation. This is one of the most critical stages of the B2B channel, where the prospect will bargain on various terms of the deal and cite details of proposals submitted by the marketer's competitors. This is the stage where the salesperson's negotiation skills are tested. There could be multiple meetings with the prospect to negotiate the final terms of the order. The salesperson has to ensure that the prospect raises an order with the best possible and favorable terms. At the same time, the prospect should be satisfied with the business terms.

## 2.3.6 Purchase order and order fulfillment

After the above stage, the prospect may finally place an order for the products or services through a Purchase Order (PO) or Release Order (RO), based on which the marketer proceeds with the order fulfillment process.

## 2.3.7 Payment Collection

The salesperson must ensure that the payment for the executed order is collected from the customer on the due date. No sale can be said to be complete till the customer releases the payment in full for the goods supplied or services rendered by the seller.

# 2.4 Business to Government (B2G) Channel

The Business to Government (B2G) channel refers to the supply of products to government organizations. The sales process to secure an order from the government organizations is as illustrated in Figure 2.8.

| Figure 2.8 | **Six Steps of B2G Sales Channel** |

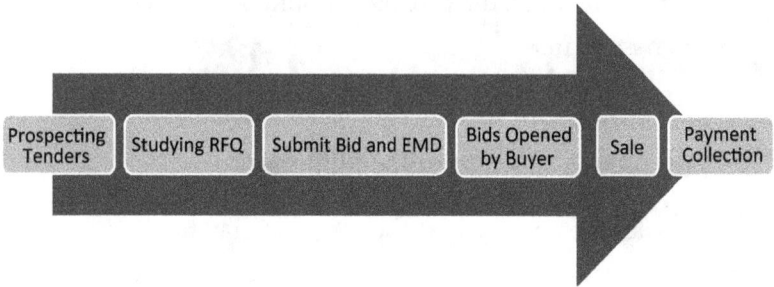

Prospecting Tenders → Studying RFQ → Submit Bid and EMD → Bids Opened by Buyer → Sale → Payment Collection

i. Such organizations release a tender notice along with RFP (Request for Proposal) or Request for Quotation (RFQ) to purchase goods or services. These documents mention all the details of the buyer's exact procurement needs and the terms and conditions for the order.

ii. Companies intending to bid for the order have to submit their bids to the prospect before the due date. Along with the bid, an Earnest Money Deposit (EMD) has to be paid to the prospect. This ensures that only serious and capable bidders participate in the tender process.

iii. The bidder has to submit various statutory documents along with the bid, like business and tax registration certificates, quality assurance certificates, details and proof of similar projects/orders executed in the past for other clients.

iv. The work order for the supply of goods/services is then awarded to the company which quotes the lowest bid. The company has to complete the assigned work or supply the goods as per the terms and conditions mentioned in the RFP/RFQ. The prospect retains the EMD of the lowest bidder as a security deposit towards the due performance of the contract. Other bidders are returned their EMD.

v. After the seller fulfills the work or supplies the products, the EMD is returned to the seller and the due payment for the work executed or goods supplied is released. If the seller fails to deliver the awarded work as required, the prospect can forfeit the EMD as a non-performance penalty.

vi. The salesperson must ensure that the payment for the executed order is collected from the government administration on the due date.

Some of the advantages of B2B and B2G sales channels are as follows:

a. Since no intermediaries are involved in this channel, companies can save money on trade margins, thus increasing their profitability.

b. The sales volumes per order in this channel are higher than that of B2C channels, and hence companies can offer bulk discounted rates to the prospects.

c. The level of commercial risk involved is less than that of the B2C channel because the sales orders are processed as per the customer's specific needs.

Some of the disadvantages of B2B and B2G sales channels are as follows:

a. A marketer is not aware of the actual price quoted to the prospect by the competitors.

b. The sales process from prospecting to closing the sale is longer than that of B2C channels.

c. In the B2G channel, there is no scope for revising the price quoted to the prospect once the bid is submitted.

# 2.5 Omni Channel Distribution

In Omni Channel distribution, customers can purchase, receive, collect or return products through multiple modes at their convenience. Omni Channel distribution essentially adds place and time utility for the consumers by allowing them to manage their orders or purchases at their convenience. The goal of the Omni Channel is to reduce costs, improve transit time and delight the customer.

**Examples of Omni Channel Distribution**

a. Buying at an offline store and getting the delivery at home

b. Buying at an offline store and availing of home pick-up to return products

c. Buying online, then picking up products from an offline store

d. Buying online, then returning products at an offline store

Various ways of Omni Channel order fulfillment and accepting returns are explained in Figure 2.9.

**Figure 2.9    Omni Channel Distribution**

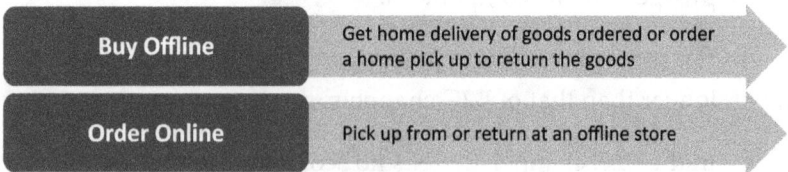

| Buy Offline | Get home delivery of goods ordered or order a home pick up to return the goods |
| Order Online | Pick up from or return at an offline store |

# Chapter Summary

◆ Companies use multiple sales and distribution channels viz; Business to Consumer (B2C), Direct to Consumer (D2C), Business to Business (B2B), Business to Government (B2G), and Omni Channel depending upon the category of products, target audience, and marketer's sales management strategy.

◆ B2C channels can be classified into intensive, selective, exclusive, television home shopping, and multi-level marketing channels.

◆ Intermediaries play a very significant role in building the distribution chain for the B2C channel.

◆ An increasing number of brands are using e-commerce platforms to exclusively sell their products through D2C channels.

◆ The B2B channel is essentially persuasion-driven and thus requires sharp negotiation skills on the salesperson's part to close the deal.

◆ B2G sales channel has a more extended gestation period from submitting the bid to the prospect to sale closure due to a lot of documentation work. Also, there is no scope for any negotiation or revision of the bid once it is submitted.

# Quiz 2

1. **The goal of distribution channels is to take products closer to the _____.**

   a. intermediaries

   b. sales agents

   c. final consumers

   d. middlemen

2. **Channels of distribution increase value for consumers by _____.**

   a. making a range of products available to them

   b. offering low prices for products

   c. raising quality of products

   d. changing the warehouse of the product

3. **Companies use intermediaries to _____.**

   a. reach the consumers in an effective manner

   b. provide best consumer offers

   c. raise their profits each year

   d. all of the above

4. **Companies rely on their intermediaries for the following information:**

   a. Consumer's buying preferences

   b. Performance of competitors

   c. What to name their products

   d. Options A & B

5. **Having intermediaries benefits companies in _____.**

   a. sharing of business risk

   b. capturing market information

   c. support during consumer promotions

   d. all of the above

6. **A distributor breaks down a bulk shipment of a product to_____.**

   a. further sell in smaller quantities and make a profit on the same

   b. pack the products in smaller quantities on behalf of the company

   c. further transport the products on behalf of the company

   d. none of the above

7. **Which of the following does not fall under the Omni channel model of distribution?**

   a. Buy a product online, then pick it up from an offline store

   b. Purchase at an offline store and get the delivery at home

   c. Buy offline and return at an offline store

   d. None of the above

8. **A retailer buys products from various manufacturers and sells them from a single store, thus increasing _____ utility for the consumers.**

   a. quantity

   b. assortment

   c. place

   d. possession

9. **_____ approach is best suited for new products whose functionality needs to be emphasized to convert the prospect into a buyer.**

   a. Gifting

   b. Question

   c. Product

   d. Persuasion

10. **Which of the following is incorrect concerning intermediaries?**

    a. They must be managed appropriately

    b. They must necessarily employ sales staff appointed by the company

    c. They should be profit-making themselves

    d. They should work in alignment with the companies' goals

| **Answers** | 1 – d | 2 – a | 3 – a | 4 – d | 5 – d |
|-------------|-------|-------|-------|-------|-------|
|             | 6 – a | 7 – d | 8 – c | 9 – c | 10 – b |

# Class Assignment

A company plans to launch packaged food products for world cuisine, including a range of organic food products, imported ingredients, and exotic foods. What kind of sales channels would be ideal for such products and why? The instructor can make a group of 4-5 students to discuss the case and share their views with the rest of the class.

# CASE STUDY:
# Tupperware in India

Kitchenware brand Tupperware started selling its products in India a couple of decades back through a network of direct sales agents who would sell the products among their social network. This was in line with its global strategy of direct selling rather than selling through traditional sales channels consisting of distributors and retailers. However, it realized that to increase its sales revenue further to match the demand potential that the Indian market offered, it would have to look at alternate and additional distribution channels.

Thus, Tupperware is foraying into the fast-growing e-commerce segment, besides having exclusive brand outlets in key cities. As per its online strategy, the company lists a majority of its product portfolios on leading e-commerce platforms like Amazon and Flipkart.

"The major drawback which we had was our access; we were not available. By addressing that, plus our investment in brand building and people, we would double our business in the next 3-4 years," Tupperware India Managing Director Deepak Chhabra said in an interview by PTI in 2019.

The firm would invest around USD 1 million (INR 7 crore) on marketing, advertising, and training its sales force or 'direct sellers' this year as it plans to open over 30 exclusive brand outlets. "This salesforce, these channels are new, and we have to train them for the next 6-8 months," he said.

Headquartered in Orlando, US, Tupperware has a turnover of USD 2.5 billion, and India is currently at the 16th position in terms of contribution to its global revenues. "Earlier India used to contribute pretty large, four-five years back...we used to be at number three in 2014," Chhabra said.

The company will utilize its existing network of direct sellers to expand its retail footprint. "Our direct sellers would be our franchise, and there would not be any capital investment from our side," he said.[3]

## Questions for discussion

Let the students research Tupperware's sales strategy in India and globally and answer the following questions:

a. Which other channels of sales & distribution should Tupperware use to increase its sales in India?

b. In which other countries has Tupperware adopted alternate distribution channels to increase the penetration of its products, and how?

---

3. Business Standard, Aug' 2019 and auto-generated from a syndicated feed

# Chapter 3

# Ensuring Product Mix in the Channel

This chapter familiarizes the students with the concept of product and brand mix and how companies can ensure that all the products, brands, and variants made available in the market are visible to the consumer. Having understood the various essential sales and distribution channels in the previous chapter, it is essential to learn how to maximize sales revenue by ensuring that the channel intermediaries sell the marketer's entire product and brand mix. Otherwise, the consumer may opt for a competitor's product even though the marketer has the same product in its catalog but is not available at the point of sale. It is thus the responsibility of the sales team to ensure that this objective is met.

Key learnings from this chapter include the reader's understanding of the following:

- What constitutes the product and brand mix of a marketer?

- What is a Stock Keeping Unit (SKU)?

- Factors that influence the mix of SKUs that needs to be maintained in the sales channel

# 3.1 Product & Brand Mix

A marketer's product and brand portfolio can be classified as illustrated in Figure 3.1.

**Figure 3.1**    **Classification of Product and Brand Mix**

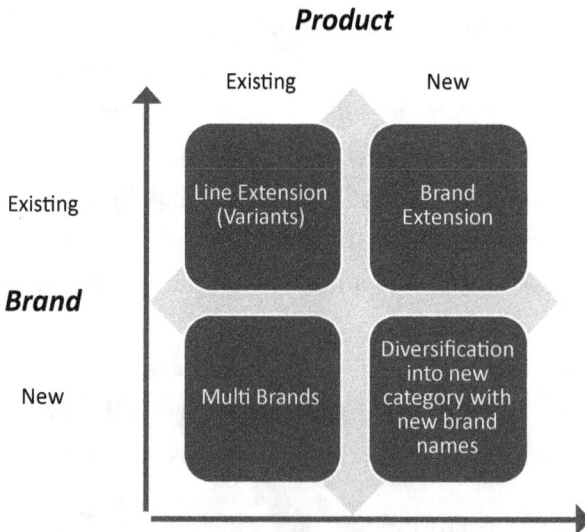

**Source:** Adapted from *Tauber's Growth Matrix*, 1981

Figure 3.2 lists examples from the brand and product portfolio of FMCG major Unilever to substantiate the said theory.

| Figure 3.2 | Product and Brand Portfolio of Unilever |

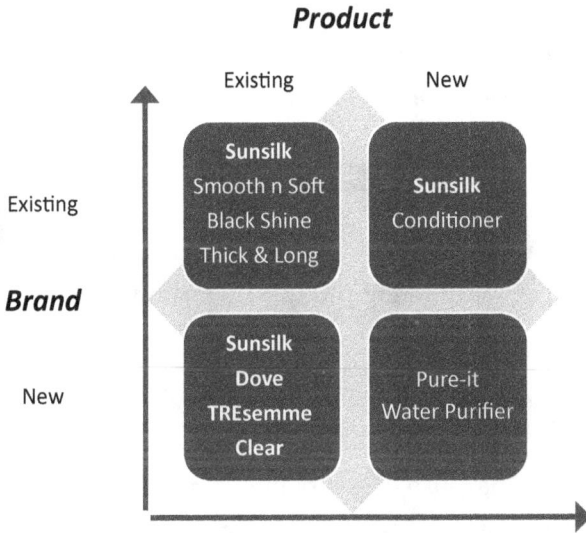

**Product**

| | Existing | New |
|---|---|---|
| Existing | **Sunsilk** Smooth n Soft Black Shine Thick & Long | **Sunsilk** Conditioner |
| New | **Sunsilk** **Dove** **TREsemme** **Clear** | Pure-it Water Purifier |

**Brand** *(vertical axis label)*

**Source:** www.unilever.com and www.hul.co.in. Based on *Tauber's Growth Matrix*, 1981

## 3.1.1 Line Extension (Variants):

The strategy of launching multiple variants for an existing brand within the existing product category is called Line Extension. The variants can be as per attributes like color, design, shape, or fragrance. E.g., Unilever has multiple variants for Sunsilk Shampoo in its portfolio, viz: Smooth & Soft, Black Shine, and Thick & Long for various hair solutions depending on individual consumers' preferences.

## 3.1.2 Multi-Brands:

The strategy of having multiple brands in the same product category to cater to the varied needs of consumers is called Multi Brands strategy. E.g., Unilever has multiple brands of shampoos in its portfolio viz: Sunsilk, Dove, TREsemme and Clear.

## 3.1.3 Brand Extension:

A marketer can use an existing brand name for launching new product categories. For example, Unilever has Sunsilk Hair Conditioner, where an existing brand (Sunsilk) has been extended to launch a new or different product (hair conditioner).

## 3.1.4 Diversification:

Companies may also diversify into entirely new product categories using a new brand name. E.g., Unilever's Indian subsidiary has diversified into water purifiers (a new product category) with a new brand called Pureit.

Considering the above, a salesperson has to ensure that the intermediaries of the marketer carry all product categories, brands, and variants so that its product catalog is fully represented and offered to the consumers at the point of sale. This helps reduce the notional loss of sales revenue if the consumer chooses a competitor's product or brand if the marketer's products are not available at the point of sale.

# 3.2 Maintaining Ideal SKU Mix

At the same time, a marketer has to ensure that all its SKUs (Stock Keeping Units) are available at the point of sale, be it at an offline retail store or an online portal. A SKU is a distinct unit of a product offering based on brand name, variant, and pack size. For example, a marketer can have six SKUs each of Brand A and Brand B, as illustrated in Figure 3.3 and Figure 3.4, respectively.

**Figure 3.3** **SKU mix for Brand A**

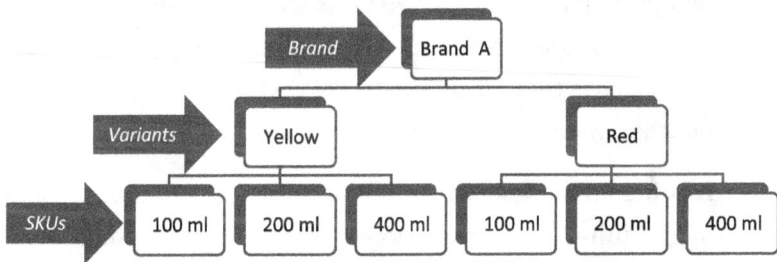

**Figure 3.4** **SKU mix for Brand B**

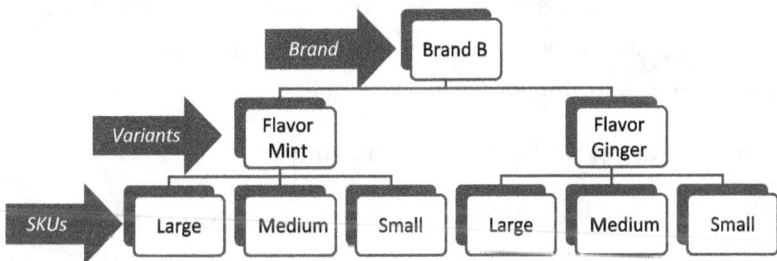

The ideal mix of SKUs that should be made available at the point of sale depends on the following factors:

a. **The demographic mix of the market**

   **Age:** Bigger pack size SKUs of a product are likely to sell more in a market where there are a large number of senior citizens as they may not be in a position to make frequent purchases. Thus, they prefer to stock up more product quantities in large pack sizes rather than frequently buying smaller sizes (e.g., Milk cartons, adult diapers, ketchup, and jam).

   **Gender:** In a market where the male population is relatively higher than females, the SKU mix should include more quantity of brand variants meant for consumption by men. This is true for products like deodorants, perfumes, watches, men's contraceptives, and shaving razors.

   **Income:** In markets where the per capita disposable income of consumers is relatively lower than that in other markets, the SKU mix may have a more significant proportion of smaller pack sizes for product categories like personal care products, home care, and fabric care. In many countries, shampoos, detergents, and hair oil are sold in small sachets containing less quantity of the product (i.e., 10 ml, ten gms), especially in rural areas or markets where people earn daily wages and thus prefer to buy smaller packs SKUs daily.

b. **Frequency and volume of consumption**

   Some products have a very high frequency or volume of consumption and hence are sold in larger pack sizes available at discounted prices. For example, grocery products, dishwashing gels, floor cleaners are also sold in mega packs in markets where the average family size is greater than that in other markets. Similarly, protein shakes, pet food, and sanitary pads are sold in large packs size SKUs.

c. **Topography of the market area**

In hilly areas, remote locations or regions with heavy snowfall, frequent traveling for shopping may not be feasible either due to hostile terrain or climatic condition or lack of transport facilities. Thus, consumers in such regions may prefer to buy products in large packs when they occasionally visit a base location with better penetration of shops.

d. **Category of buyers**

Buyers can be classified as individual consumers or institutional buyers. Institutional buyers refer to organizations that buy products for use by their employees. Some of these products are stationery, tea and sugar sachets, and office consumables. Thus, in a Central Business District (CBD), a commercial or a business hub, marketers may see better off-take of larger pack size SKUs as institutional buyers prefer to buy products in bulk quantity.

e. **Individual buying preferences**

Different consumers have different tastes, likes, and buying preferences depending on the solution they are looking for to meet their needs. Thus a marketer needs to be aware of their needs to decide on the ideal SKU mix. For example, some consumers look for detergents that leave fragrance on the clothes for long hours. Some consumers look for detergents that are soft on the fabric while washing the clothes. A marketer should analyze the sales data of each market to identify if any pattern of consumption emerges based on the SKU sales. Accordingly, the marketer has to ensure that the proportion of relevant SKUs is maintained in the sales channel at all times. For example, if a particular market has many Asians living there, SKUs of ready-to-eat Asian cuisine may see higher sales than other cuisines.

f. **Sales promotions by the marketer**

During sales promotions the SKU mix should also include trial packs, introductory packs, and discounted combo packs introduced by the marketer so that its products get added to the consideration set of the consumers.

The marketer has to analyze the sales pattern of its various products, brands, variants to arrive at the right mix of SKUs that needs to be maintained in the sales channel, along with optimum inventory level for each SKU so that consumers can include the marketer's products in their consideration set while making a purchase decision.

# Chapter Summary

◆ Marketers with a comprehensive catalog of products, brands, variants, and brand extension products should maintain visibility for their entire assortment of SKUs in the sales channel.

◆ The ideal mix and inventory level of each SKU that has to be maintained in the sales channel of a particular market depends on various factors that influence the consumers' buying preferences in that market.

◆ Analysis of the sales pattern of each SKU in a particular market area helps marketers arrive at the optimum inventory level to be maintained in the sales channel.

# Quiz 3

1. P&G's brands include Head & Shoulders-Cool Menthol and Head & Shoulders-Anti Hair fall. What is this strategy called?

   a. Multi Brands

   b. Line Extension

   c. Brand Extension

   d. Solo Brand

2. Unilever sells Lux and Lifebuoy soaps. Which strategy is this?

   a. Multi Brands

   b. Line Extension

   c. Brand Extension

   d. Diversification

3. Reckitt sells Dettol antiseptic, hand sanitizer, and hand wash. Which strategy is this?

   a. Multi Brands

   b. Line Extension

   c. Brand Extension

   d. Diversification

4. GSK forayed into the noodles category with Horlicks Foodles in the Indian market. Which strategy is this?

   a. Multi Brands

   b. Line Extension

   c. Brand Extension

   d. Diversification

5. What does the abbreviation SKU stand for?

   a. Stock Keeping User

   b. Stock Keeping Unit

   c. Stock Known Unit

   d. None of the above

For questions 6 and 7, see Figure 3.5, which lists the product catalog of a marketer.

**Product catalog of a marketer**

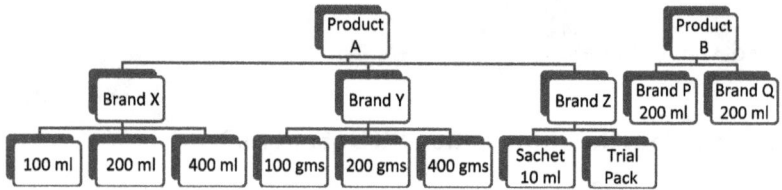

6. Total number of SKUs of the marketer is:

    a. 8

    b. 10

    c. 5

    d. 6

7. For Product A the marketer is following which strategy:

    a. Brand Extension

    b. Variants

    c. Multi Brands

    d. Diversification

An apparel manufacturer's product catalog is given in Figure 3.6. Answer questions 8-10 considering the same.

| Figure 3.6 | An apparel manufacturer's product catalog |

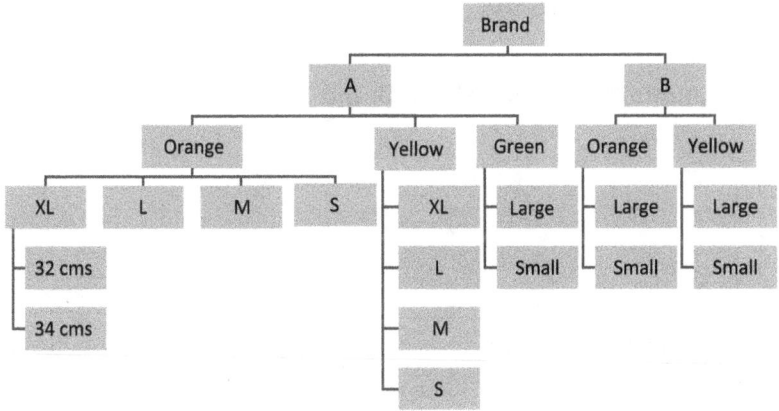

8. Total number of SKUs is:

   a. 15

   b. 14

   c. 5

   d. 2

9. **Total number of variants for Brand A is:**

    a. 3

    b. 8

    c. 9

    d. None of the above

10. **Total number of variants for Brand B is:**

    a. 2

    b. 4

    c. 6

    d. None of the above

| **Answers** | 1 – b | 2 – a | 3 – c | 4 – d | 5 – b |
|---|---|---|---|---|---|
| | 6 – b | 7 – c | 8 – a | 9 – a | 10 – a |

# Field assignment for students

The instructor can make a group of 3 students each. Each group should understand the complete SKU mix of a particular brand and then visit any three offline/online stores that sell the said brand of products. Students should then analyze the gaps observed by them in the SKU mix present at these stores. Such gap analysis should be based on the factors that influence the ideal SKU mix to be maintained at the point of sale.

# CASE STUDY:
# Optimizing Product, Brand, and SKU mix of an online portal

An online shopping portal in India is changing its business strategy. As a result, the company has optimized its category, brand, and SKU mix to suit consumer needs. There is a need to evaluate the performance of all categories to ensure that the respective category's brand and SKU mix offers maximum sales opportunities in sync with the demographic factors of its consumer base. At present, several factors are responsible for under optimization of product and brand mix, which include the following:

- A micro-level decentralized inventory holding strategy for every cluster of 15-mile radius from the last mile of order fulfillment (i.e., a consumer's location). This resulted in the stocking of varying product and brand mixes (i.e., the mix of categories, brands, and SKUs varied for each cluster)

- Critical and essential product sub-categories and/or variants were not stocked in some clusters, whereas they were over-stocked in other clusters

- Brand/SKU selection was not in sync with consumer demographics (i.e., likes, preferences, tastes, seasonal demand, trends)

- The product and brand mix, specific to regional market requirement and demand, was not being optimized in many regions and had a consistent shortage of fast-moving SKUs

- Some clusters were having SKUs that were older than 30 days

The portal has hired you as a consultant to evaluate several categories like Food & Grocery, Healthcare & Beauty, General Merchandise, Convenience Goods, etc., and to give product mix optimization recommendations. What will be your recommendations?

## Suggested Solution:

India is a market with varied regional disparities in consumer buying behavior due to several factors influencing consumers' buying decisions. The tastes and preferences of consumers here differ almost every few hundred miles. The consumer's choice for most of the products on an online shopping portal largely depends on the mix of the following demographic and geographic factors:

Income, religion, language, age, sex, education, festivals or celebratory occasions, marital status, occupation, family size, and climatic condition.

Considering the above, to develop recommendations for an improved product mix, it is necessary to understand the following:

- The relation matrix between the consumer demographics, product demographics, and consumer profile data to ensure that the recommended product mix is aligned with the customer mix.

- The consumer's buying pattern (i.e., the average frequency of buying, quantity ordered and cart value for each order).

- Inflection points when the demand for specific SKUs increases (i.e., discount offers, festive season, weekends, holidays, new product launch, or pay days) or decreases during weekdays or price increase of SKUs.

- The average order fulfillment cycle of the suppliers for each SKU so that inventory is replenished in time.

Based on the above data and analysis, the product, brand, and assortment mix for each cluster can be identified. The recommendations can include the following:

- Determination of the categories, brands, and variants to carry for each cluster

- Suggested SKUs to stock for each cluster

- Including regional brands and SKUs that address the local market's tastes and preferences

- The use of relevant software to estimate the market demand

In addition to the above recommendations:

- The client needs to adopt a centralized approach to stock national brands, which are uniform across markets.

- Each cluster can be permitted to stock products with strong local appeal. This approach can also result in negotiating favorable terms of trade with suppliers.

# Chapter **4**

# Product Selling to Concept Selling

Over the years, there has been a change in how marketers approach the selling process. There has been a shift from selling products and services to selling a concept. This chapter explains what is meant by 'concept selling' and how it is different from product selling with the help of relevant examples. Readers will also be familiarized with the theory and practice of 'Concept Selling' and how a marketer can use this approach to build a value proposition for the consumers or prospects.

Key learnings from this chapter include the reader's understanding of the following:

- Importance of shifting from product selling to concept selling

- How to help the consumers in planning their need fulfillment hierarchy

- Offering the prospect not just a need fulfillment solution but also an opportunity to achieve a sense of fulfillment

Concept Selling goes one step ahead of product selling. It is not just about fulfilling the current needs of the consumers but also about selling an idea that fulfills the future needs of the consumers as well. It also involves meeting the aspirational wants of the consumers in advance and providing solutions to meet the peripheral needs around their primary needs. Concept selling is about selling a story that the prospects can relate to— a story that revolves around the prospect's need hierarchy.

## 4.1 Shift from product selling to concept selling

Product selling involves providing tangible and intangible values to the consumers to satisfy their stated needs with pre-defined expectations. However concept selling involves making the consumers believe in an idea or a concept rather than selling them a solution of which they are already aware. Concept selling helps consumers visualize their future needs and secure a solution. It is not about selling the technical specifications of the offering but about creating a Unique Selling Proposition (USP) that addresses their current needs, future needs, peripheral needs, and aspirational needs. These needs can be either stated or unstated. Thus, the concept selling approach is illustrated in Figure 4.1.

---
**Figure 4.1**   **Concept Selling Approach**
---

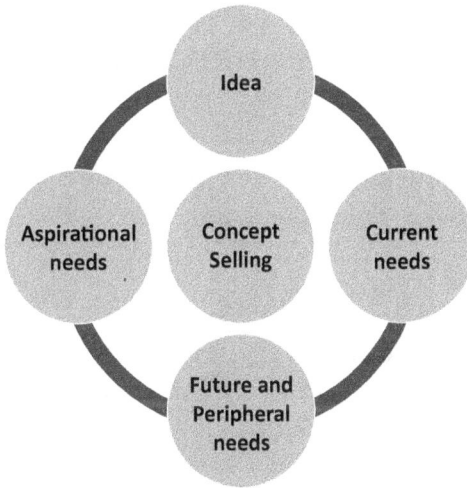

Let us understand some of the examples of concept selling.

## Living Apartments to Community Living

Many housing projects in urban areas are no longer sold as living apartments; they are sold as Community Living concepts that offer integrated housing with life-enhancing benefits. In many countries, housing projects are sold as a concept offering gated community living with owned apartments and shared amenities. In community living, residents live among like-minded individuals, share common facilities, participate in community events, have quick access to shopping, dining, education, entertainment, and other lifestyle destinations. At the same time, residents can use shared resources like a fitness center, swimming pool, sports arena, jogger's track, cycling track, concierge services, security services, and many more. Most importantly, residents have an opportunity to make new friends. Moreover, the residents are connected through an app that offers intelligent solutions like ordering daily needs from a nearby store, approving entry for visitors, raising complaints to the community office, booking appointments for the fitness center, and paying bills. Planet Smartcity is one such service that provides innovative solutions to large community living projects. The concept of community living is illustrated in Figure 4.2.

**Figure 4.2**    **Concept of Community Living**

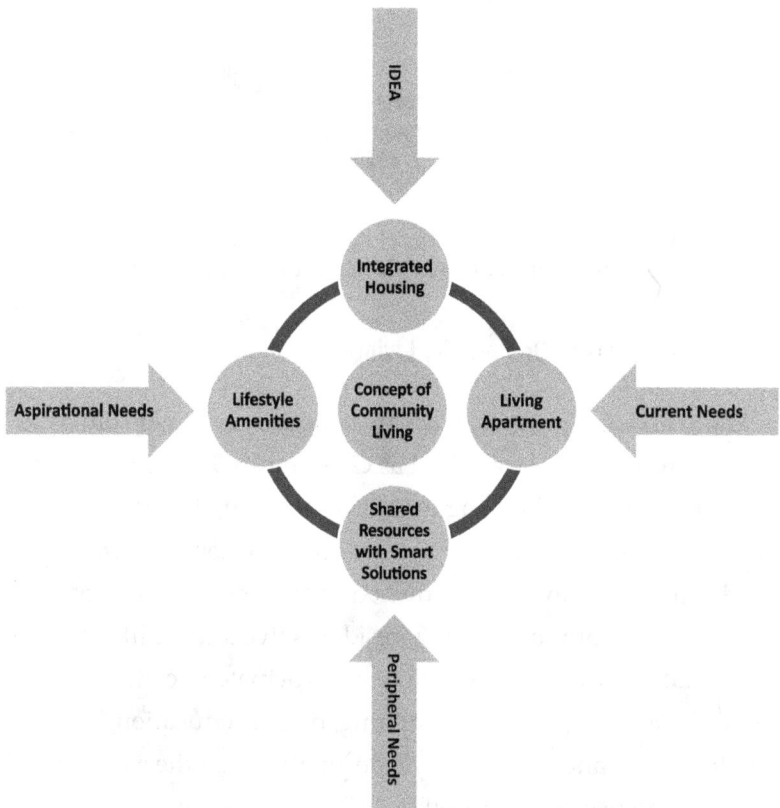

## Sports Tickets to Sports Tourism

Major sporting events like The Olympics and the Sports World Cup are now being marketed and sold as a package of live entertainment, leisure travel, shopping experience, and destination tourism. In association with tour package operators, the organizers bundle these experiences as a single product offering. The reason for this trend is that people no longer want to be glued to television screens. As urban living becomes increasingly hectic, viewers prefer to bundle all these activities in a single holiday to make the most of the little free time they get from their busy schedules. The viewers get an opportunity to witness the gala event and buy souvenirs, attend post-event parties, and visit tourist places. Sports tourism is all about this concept of integrated experiences —not just about sport, but a matter of short holidays where supporters become sports tourists. The concept of sports tourism is illustrated in Figure 4.3.

| Figure 4.3 | Concept of Sports Tourism |

## Insurance Products to Financial Security

Insurance service providers also use concept selling rather than selling the insurance policy directly. They sell the idea of 'financial security' to the prospect. The insurance policy is sold to satisfy one's need for financial security in case of any unfortunate event that may adversely impact the insured's financial position. Some insurance policies also promise continued financial support for the insured's family, thus fulfilling their future financial needs like the cost of education for the children or a monthly payout to the insured's family after one's death. Thus, the insured is sold the idea of creating a 'protective financial shield' for the family during one's absence. The concept of financial security for selling insurance products is illustrated in Figure 4.4.

<table>
<tr><td>Figure 4.4</td><td>Concept of Financial Security</td></tr>
</table>

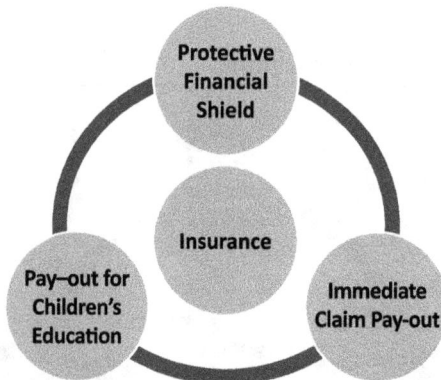

## Hotel Rooms to Destination Weddings

Heritage Hotels, Royal Palace Hotels, and Luxury Hotels in scenic locations increasingly use concept selling to enhance their room occupancy levels. These hotels offer a complete package of wedding services, including accommodation and transportation arrangements for the guests and the couple, venue in the hotel for a wedding ceremony, food and beverages, decoration of the venue, etc. The idea behind this concept called 'Destination

Wedding' is that the couple and their family are relieved of the hassles of organizing these arrangements and have more time at their disposal to enjoy the event. The concept of the destination wedding is illustrated in Figure 4.5.

| Figure 4.5 | Concept of Destination Wedding |

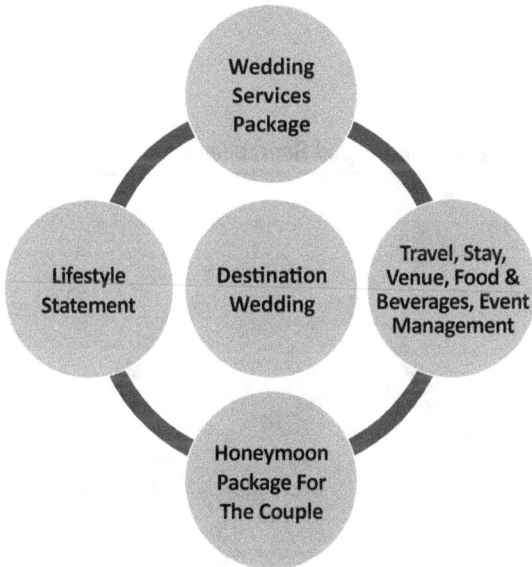

## Sports and Recreation Club Membership

Selling a membership of sports and recreation clubs can also be considered concept selling. The idea proposition being sold here is that the club membership is a solution to meet the following needs of its patrons:

a. Sports entertainment, leisure, and dining (stated and current needs)

b. Access to luxury sports (future and aspirational need)

c. Social networking (unstated need)

Sports clubs broadly position themselves as a venue for playing sports and a destination that offers an opportunity to network among other members from similar or higher socio-economic classes. At the same time, members get access to luxury sports which is an aspirational need. The concept of sports and recreation clubs is illustrated in Figure 4.6.

**Figure 4.6**   **Concept of Sports and Recreation Club**

## 4.2 Advantages of concept selling

a. The focus of the sales pitch shifts from selling a product to making things easier, hassle-free and effort-free.

b. It can be positioned as a package that fulfills the prospect's stated and unstated, and aspirational needs.

c. The prospect broadly evaluates the cost-benefit-value equation of the entire package rather than evaluating the value received for each of the products or services.

d. The package may be customized as per the prospects' requirements based on their needs and budget.

## Chapter Summary

◆ Concept selling revolves around pitching an idea that is a solution for a prospect's existing, future, and aspirational needs.

◆ There is a shift from product selling to concept selling, especially when the consumers are looking for a mix of tangible and intangible products and services.

◆ In concept selling, the salesperson has to focus on the convenience value offered to the prospect rather than the pricing of each of the elements of the product or service offering.

# Quiz 4

1. Concept selling includes _____.

   a. fulfilling the existing needs of the consumers

   b. fulfilling the future needs of the consumers

   c. meeting the aspirational wants of the consumers

   d. all of the above

2. Concept selling is about selling to the prospects a story which _____.

   a. they can relate to

   b. revolves around their need hierarchy

   c. both A & B

   d. none of the above

3. A marketer can use 'Concept Selling' to _____.

   a. build a value proposition for the prospects

   b. help the prospects in planning their need fulfillment journey

   c. help the prospects achieve a sense of fulfillment

   d. all of the above

**4. Which of the following is a part of concept selling?**

    a. Fulfilling peripheral needs around primary needs

    b. Tertiary needs

    c. Unknown needs

    d. All of the above

**5. Which of the following is true about concept selling?**

    a. Selling the technical specifications of the product

    b. Selling a Unique Selling Proposition

    c. Both A & B

    d. All of the above

**6. Many housing projects in urban areas are sold as_____.**

    a. community living concepts

    b. integrated housing projects

    c. providing life-enhancing benefits

    d. all of the above

**7. Sports events nowadays are sold as a package of _____.**

    a. live entertainment

    b. destination tourism

    c. leisure travel

    d. all of the above

8. **Insurance service providers use concept selling to sell the idea of _____.**

   a. financial security

   b. protective financial shield

   c. both A & B

   d. none of the above

9. **The concept of Destination Wedding includes providing the following services _____.**

   a. accommodation for guests

   b. transportation for guests

   c. venue for the wedding

   d. all of the above

10. **Which of the following is not an advantage of concept selling?**

    a. Making things hassle-free for the prospect

    b. It can be customized as per the prospect's requirement

    c. Prospect can be overcharged

    d. None of the above

| **Answers** | 1 – d | 2 – c | 3 – d | 4 – a | 5 – b |
|---|---|---|---|---|---|
| | 6 – d | 7 – d | 8 – c | 9 – d | 10 – c |

# CASE STUDY:
# Apple's conceptual selling of its ecosystem

### Do not Sell Products, Sell Dreams...

Apple's strategy involves selling its consumers a global package of dreams, personal experiences, and status, and it makes almost all other products go unnoticed if they do not carry the Apple logo. Apple managed to reinvent products that were already on the market. When someone purchases an Apple product, you are not only buying a great piece of modern technology; you are buying a little piece of ideology to put in your pocket. By carrying it, you adopt Steve Jobs's visions: dreams can be fulfilled, take a position in life and stand up for it, do not squander your life living by someone else's rules. Be true to yourself.

Apple is different from all other brands because, for Steve Jobs, consumers were not just consumers; they were people. People with dreams, hopes, and ambitions got Apple to create products to help them achieve their dreams and goals. Apple focuses on creating a universe of sensations, experiences, and values that people get when they buy an Apple product. When you purchase an Apple MacBook Air, you are not only buying a computer where you can do your work, edit pics, videos, and connect with friends and family. You buy Apple's belief that people with passion can change the world and make it a better place.[4]

---

4. Excerpts from https://postcron.com/en/blog/10-amazing-marketing-lessons-steve-jobs-taught-us/

**Why Apple Is Still a Great Marketer and What You Can Learn from it...**

Create an Experience Ecosystem. Apple has a legendary focus on the customer experience. Every customer touchpoint (products, the website, ads, app store, and retail store) yields a consistent Apple experience. Over the last ten years, Apple has aggressively expanded the Apple experience areas part of daily life. By encouraging app builders but rigidly enforcing standards, Apple ensures that the universe of Apple-mediated behaviors continually expands. By innovating product form factor and function, from computing in either your pocket or on your wrist to pay for all your purchases, to opening your hotel room, to controlling all of your home electronics, to reminding you of your calorie count or parking spot... all of these experiences are connected, integrated, and packaged in a singular accessible ecosystem of complementary products. Additionally, Apple has focused on innovation beyond the core by creating the infrastructure to enable this ecosystem securely and seamlessly (think Apple Pay secure payments or biometric facial recognition on the iPhone X). The most tangible example, of course, is in Apple stores. Apple overturned conventional retailing wisdom when it created its stores, putting experience before "selling." It is continually building on that success by removing "store" from its retail branding because it sees its stores as so much more.[5]

Based on the above case, explain how 'Apple does not sell products, but it sells an idea or a concept.'

---

5. Excerpts from https://www.forbes.com/sites/christinemoorman/2018/01/12/why-apple-is-still-a-great-marketer-and-what-you-can-learn/?sh=152d0e8415bd

## Solution

The reader should be able to depict and elaborate Apple's concept selling approach as illustrated in Figure 4.7.

**Figure 4.7**  **Apple's concept selling approach**

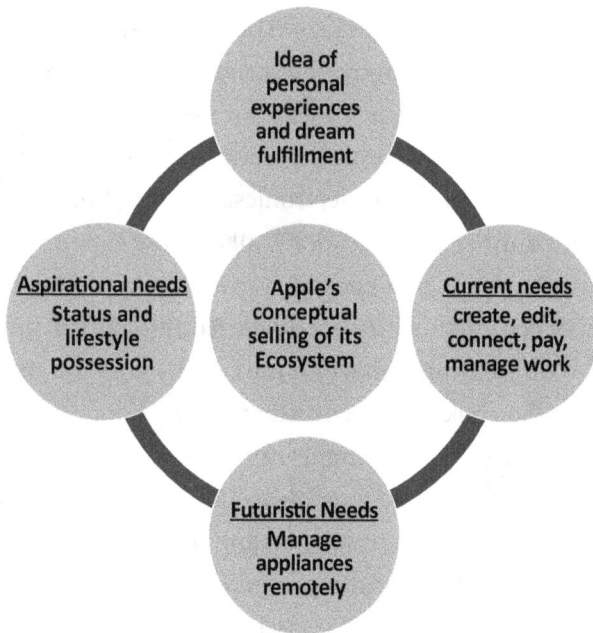

- Idea of personal experiences and dream fulfillment
- Aspirational needs: Status and lifestyle possession
- Apple's conceptual selling of its Ecosystem
- Current needs: create, edit, connect, pay, manage work
- Futuristic Needs: Manage appliances remotely

# Chapter 5

# Push v/s Pull Strategy

One of the most common dilemmas that marketers face is whether to reach out to the consumers or to make them reach out to the marketers. This chapter will help the readers address this dilemma by familiarizing them with the Push and Pull strategies that marketers adopt to sell their products or services in the market. Readers will also understand the difference between both these approaches and when to adopt each of these approaches. They will also get a perspective on the theory and practice of Push and Pull strategies.

Key learnings from this chapter include the reader's understanding of the following:

- Difference between Push and Pull strategies that generate demand for products and services

- Features, advantages, and disadvantages of Push and Pull strategies

- Conditions under which each of these strategies can be adopted

All marketing and sales efforts can be classified under two broad categories: Push or Pull. These are the two promotional strategies that are used to ensure that the product reaches its target market. In Push sales strategy, the objective is to push the company's products into the sales channels through intermediaries. These intermediaries further push the products into the consumer's consideration set by making them aware of the products at the point of sale. On the other hand, the pull strategy is about 'making the consumers come to you for the products.' The two types of strategies, thus, differ in the way consumers are approached.

## 5.1 Push Strategy

Push strategy is wherein intermediaries, i.e., distributors and retailers, are engaged to aggressively push the product or service into the sales channel so that the end consumer invariably notices the product. This strategy aims to take the product to the last mile, i.e., end consumers, who may not be familiar with the product. Alternatively, the product might not be in their consideration set. This strategy uses various trade promotional activities like the point of sale display, direct selling, participating in trade fairs and exhibitions, sampling, product trials, discounts on introductory packs, lucky draws, and contests at the point of sale. The idea is to proactively push the product into the consumer's consideration set while making a purchase decision and reduce the time between product discovery and purchase.

# 5.2 Pull Strategy

Pull strategy, on the other hand, aims at creating a pull for the product offering, such that the target audience demands the product or service from the channel partners. In this strategy, consumer demand is generated by creating awareness for the product through advertising efforts. The product thus forms a part of the consumer's consideration set. The product is advertised across television networks, print media, radio stations, hoardings, digital and social media platforms, and through product placement in movies and television shows, resulting in 'pull' demand for the products. However, the strategy requires a considerable amount of advertising budget to create noise for the product in a market that is already cluttered with a plethora of brands. Moreover, with the evolution of multiple advertising platforms, reaching the target audience requires consistent and frequent advertising for the product during the initial launch phase. This further increases the advertising budget for the marketer.

Thus, the fundamental difference between Push and Pull strategies can be illustrated as in Figure 5.1.

**Figure 5.1**  **Push Strategy v/s Pull Strategy**

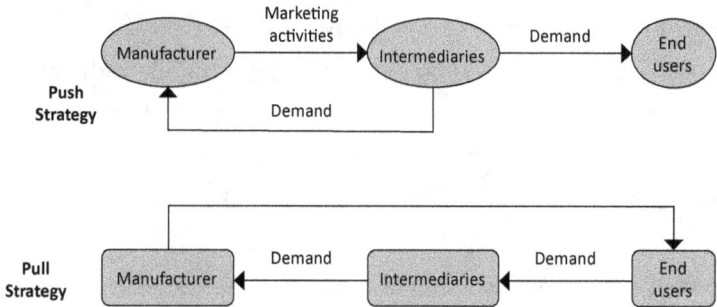

**Source:** https://mpk732t12016clusterb.wordpress.com/2016/05/16/hewlett-packards-push-pull-strategy/

# 5.3 Difference between Push and Pull Strategies

The difference between the features of Push and Pull strategies are characterized based on the objectives to be met, the approach adopted and tools used to meet the said objectives, allocation of organizational resources, and other factors as outlined in Table 5.1.

| Table 5.1 | Difference between Push and Pull Strategies |
| --- | --- |

|  | Push Strategy | Pull Strategy |
| --- | --- | --- |
| **Meaning & Objective** | To create awareness for the product and push it into the consideration set of the end consumers primarily through sales efforts directed towards the channel intermediaries. | To create awareness for the product and generate demand for it primarily through advertising efforts directed towards the end consumers. |
| **Approach** | Channel intermediaries have to be persuaded and provided incentives to stock and push the company's products into the end **consumer's consideration** set. | Awareness and interest for the product are created by pro-actively advertising it among the target audience. The product, thus, enters the **consumers' consideration** set, and they demand it from the intermediaries. |
| **Tools used to achieve the objectives** | Trade promotion activities like:<br>• Offering more trade margins to channel partners to push the products further in the channel<br>• Creating an aggressive point of sale display to increase the visibility of the product<br>• Using attractive product packaging for increased product visibility at the point of sale<br>• Participating in trade fairs & exhibitions to introduce the product<br>• Target based incentives for channel partners<br>• Giving high and exclusive discounts on products to major offline/online retailers | Advertising and consumer promotion activities like:<br>• Advertisements across TV networks, print publications, websites, radio, out-of-home media, etcetera.<br>• Product placement in movies and reality shows<br>• Sponsoring live events, award shows, college fests<br>• Scratch card offers, lucky draws, contests.<br>• Coupons and price offs<br>• Free branded merchandise with the product<br>• Distributing free samples and trial packs. |

|  | Push Strategy | Pull Strategy |
| --- | --- | --- |
| **When and Why to use** | • Introducing a new product requires either educating the consumers about its features and benefits or product demonstration. E.g., industrial machines, innovative appliances, scratch removal kits for cars.<br><br>• Persuading the intermediaries to stock enough quantity of the product before a pull strategy is executed to meet potential demand generated by the pull strategy.<br><br>• When brand loyalty and product differentiation are low, sales intermediaries can influence consumers' choices. Thus, the product has to be pushed to the intermediaries by offering them better terms of trade. E.g., commodities like bullion, bulk drugs offer low product differentiation. | • While launching a new product for which aggressive advertising is done to reach the target audience. This creates awareness and interest for the product, and thus it enters the consumers' consideration set while making a purchase decision. Hence pull demand is generated without much dependence on the channel intermediaries.<br><br>• While launching new products/brand extensions under the parent or umbrella brand. Here the consumer is already aware of the brand, and the advertising campaign acts as a catalyst for the brand to get included in the consumer's consideration set. |

| | Push Strategy | Pull Strategy |
|---|---|---|
| **When and Why to use** | • For products where price may be the only deciding factor for the end consumer in a fiercely competitive market. Hence, incentivizing the sales channel intermediaries is required to push sales.<br>• When market demand for the product category is less than supply due to unfavorable market conditions. Hence, push strategy helps maintain or increase sales revenue.<br>• For product categories that are either not allowed to be advertised by law or have a price cap. Thus, the pull strategy cannot be used (e.g., tobacco products, liquor, essential commodities, legal services). | • In a highly competitive market that requires high advertising spending to get noticed by the target audience, among the clutter of brands. This ensures that the marketer's brand is in the consideration set of the end consumers while making a purchase decision.<br>• When loyalty for competing brands is high among the target audience, aggressive advertising efforts are required to maintain brand recall for the marketer's brand.<br>• For reducing dependence on channel intermediaries for demand generation |
| **Promotional Budget** | Higher allocation towards incentivizing sales channel intermediaries | Higher allocation for consumer-oriented advertising and promotions |
| **Business Terms** | Channel intermediaries may have better negotiation and bargaining power than marketers | Marketers may have better negotiation and bargaining power than channel intermediaries |
| **Resource Allocation** | Resources are allocated mainly towards sales efforts | Resources are primarily allocated towards advertising efforts |

# 5.4 Advantages and Disadvantages of Push and Pull Strategies

While deciding which strategy has to be followed, the marketers should consider the advantages and disadvantages of both the strategies as outlined in Table 5.2.

| Table 5.2 | Advantages and disadvantages of Push and Pull Strategies |
| --- | --- |

| | Advantages | Disadvantages |
| --- | --- | --- |
| Push | • Less lead time to introduce a new product in the market because consumer-oriented promotions may not be required<br>• Low sales & marketing budgets are required because high advertising spends are not be needed<br><br>• More flexibility to increase product's retail price to offer more trade margins to the channel intermediaries | • Since consumer awareness for the product is low due to a lack of consumer-oriented promotional activities, marketers have to depend on channel intermediaries to generate demand.<br><br>Hence sales intermediaries have better bargaining power for negotiating trade terms in their favor.<br>• Data and information about consumer behavior may not be readily available if channel intermediaries are hesitant to share the same.<br>• Less opportunity to build brand recall among end Consumers due to lack of consumer-oriented promotional activities |

| | Advantages | Disadvantages |
|---|---|---|
| **Pull** | • Better negotiation power for business terms than that of sales intermediaries as consumers proactively seek the product due to consumer-oriented promotions. Thus, dependence on channel partners is low. | • High lead time to introduce a new product in the market as consumer-oriented promotional activities have to be planned and executed well in advance |
| | • Opportunity to build brand recall among the target audience due to consumer-oriented promotional activities | • High-cost proposition as marketing spends have to be allocated for advertising besides trade promotional budgets. |

It is imperative to understand that in practice, both the strategies may have interdependence to some extent. However, the equation of interdependence varies based on an organization's internal policies, market conditions, and stage of the product life cycle.

## Chapter Summary

◆ Both Push and Pull strategies are used to create awareness and demand for products. While the Push strategy relies more on the channel intermediaries to generate sales revenue, the Pull strategy relies more on consumer-oriented advertising to create awareness of the product among the target audience.

◆ Push strategy involves providing sales incentives to the channel intermediaries, whereas Pull strategy focuses more on attracting the target audience.

◆ None of the strategies can be used in complete isolation for all practical purposes as there is bound to be some interdependence between them.

# Quiz 5

1. **Which of the following are characteristics of Push strategy?**

   a. Pushing products into the sales channels through intermediaries

   b. Intermediaries push the product into the consumer's consideration set

   c. Making consumers aware of the products at the point of sale

   d. All of the above

2. **Which of the following are characteristics of the Pull strategy?**

   a. Attracting consumers come to purchase products or services

   b. Awareness for the product is created through consumer-oriented advertising efforts

   c. Product may be already in the consideration set of the consumer while making a purchase decision

   d. All of the above

3. **Which of the following is not valid for the Pull strategy?**

   a. Advertising the product is not required

   b. Intermediaries are not required to sell the products

   c. Both A & B

   d. None of the above

4. **Push strategy focuses on which of the following?**

   a. More incentives for the channel partners

   b. Consumer-oriented promotions

   c. More incentives for the end consumers

   d. All of the above

5. **Which of the following is not accurate for a push strategy?**

   a. Intermediaries may demand favorable terms of trade from the marketer

   b. It is used when consumers have low brand loyalty

   c. It is used when consumers have high brand loyalty

   d. Trade promotional activities are needed to push the products in the sales channel

6. **In a Pull strategy_____.**

   a. marketers tend to have better bargaining power than the intermediaries

   b. consumer awareness is not required

   c. intermediaries decide the final price of the product for the end consumers

   d. options A&C

7. **Which of the following is a trade promotion activity?**

   a. Sponsoring a live event

   b. Discount coupons for end consumers

   c. Target-based incentives for channel partners

   d. All of the above

8. **Which of the following comes under the Pull strategy?**

   a. Scratch card promotions for end consumers

   b. Participating in trade fairs

   c. Brand placement in movies

   d. Options A & C

9. **Push strategy is suitable mainly for which of the following products?**

   a. Products that cannot be advertised by law

   b. Industrial products

   c. Products for which consumers have low band loyalty

   d. All of the above

10. **A company is offering a paid holiday to its sales intermediaries who achieve their sales target. This comes under _____ strategy.**

    a. pull

    b. push

| **Answers** | 1 – d | 2 – d | 3 – c | 4 – a | 5 – c |
|-------------|-------|-------|-------|-------|-------|
|             | 6 – a | 7 – c | 8 – d | 9 – d | 10 – b |

# CASE STUDY:
# Push and Pull Strategies in the pharmaceutical industry

When it comes to using the Push or Pull strategy, the pharmaceutical market is considered an exception. In the pharmaceutical market, there are two types of medicines-prescription medicines and over-the-counter (OTC) medicines. Prescription medicines can be purchased only by presenting a valid prescription of a medical practitioner to the pharmacist. However, OTC medicines can be purchased over the counter without a prescription. For prescription medicines, an aggressive push strategy is followed during the introductory phase because the decision to purchase the medicines is not taken by the end consumer. This decision is made by the medical practitioner who prescribes the medicines to the patient based on the illness and its cure. Statutory laws in most countries do not allow advertising and promoting prescription medicines to the end consumer as he or she does not have the requisite knowledge of how the medicine works in curing the ailment. Hence all marketing and sales push efforts have to be directed towards the medical fraternity, pharmacy stores and intermediaries who supply the medicines to these stores. However, once the medicine receives statutory permission for selling it over the counter without any prescription, marketing efforts are directed towards the end consumers.

Effectively the pharmaceutical industry follows a push as well as pull strategy for selling the medicines. During the push phase, efforts are undertaken to educate the medical fraternity about how the drug works to cure the ailment, the molecular composition of the drug, the dosage required to be administered to the patients, etc. Examples of push sales activities for pharmaceutical products include giving a free sample of the product to the doctor by the medical rep, presenting articles and studies about the medicine in leading pharma journals, continuing education for doctors through conferences and symposiums. Here the role of the medical representative is very crucial and critical because he or she is the first point of contact with the doctor who can prescribe the medicine to the patients. The doctors are given a small token gift with the name and brand logo of the medicine printed on it so that brand recall is maintained. On the other hand, the product sales and distribution teams have to simultaneously sell the product to distributors and pharmacists from where the end consumers can buy the products.

Once the efficacy of the medicine to effectively cure the ailment is established, pharmaceutical companies can seek statutory approval to sell their medicines over the counter without a prescription. Once this approval is received, a pull strategy to create demand for the medicines is adopted by implementing consumer-oriented advertising and sales promotion activities.

At the same time, consumer pull strategies for prescription medicines are also adopted in some countries where pharmaceutical companies have the provision of advertising their drugs on select advertising media. This type of advertising is called Direct to Consumer Advertising (DTCA), wherein consumers are more informed about the available therapeutic options and thus, become partners in the decisions related to their health. DTCA allows consumers to buy prescription drugs after consultation with their physicians about what they have learned from the advertisements.

The pharmaceutical industry thus follows aggressive push strategies during the initial phase of product launch, and once the medicine enters the OTC segment, the focus shifts to pull activities.

# Class Assignment

Identify two other products or services that require similar push and pull strategies like the pharmaceutical products and discuss how the companies market them.

# Chapter 6

# Cross-Selling, Up-selling, Value-Added Selling

Any organization's objective is to maximize sales revenue from existing customers and by selling to new customers. This objective can be achieved through Cross-Selling, Up-Selling, and Value-Added Selling, through which marketers can increase their average revenue per customer without spending additional marketing resources. This chapter will discuss the above strategies and how each of these can be practiced by a marketer to increase sales revenue.

Key learnings for the reader from this chapter include the reader's understanding of the following:

- Meaning of cross-selling, up-selling, and value-added selling with relevant examples

- How to effectively use these sales strategies to optimize sales revenue from each customer

- Advantages of each of these strategies for the consumer and marketer

The difference between Upselling and Cross-Selling can be illustrated as in Figure 6.1.

**Figure 6.1**   **Difference between Cross-Selling and Up-Selling**

Source: https://www.wordstream.com/blog/ws/2018/05/30/cross-selling-upselling

# 6.1 Cross-Selling

Cross-Selling means persuading a customer to buy additional products that are complementary or supplementary to the product that he or she intends to buy. It involves selling additional products that gel well with the products that the customer is just about to buy by offering them the choice to buy those products at the right time within the store. Cross-selling also includes selling ancillary products or add-ons to the product that the consumer is planning to buy.

Following are some examples of cross-selling:

1.  Shirt/Trouser & Tie / Tie Pin / Belt

2.  Electronic Toy & Battery

3.  Game Console & Joystick

4.  Laptop & Anti-Virus / Printer / Computer Accessories

5.  Car & Car Accessories

6. Air Ticket & Hotel Accommodation

7. Mobile & Head Phones / Mobile Case

8. Printer & Ink Refill Cartridge

9. Hair Dryer & Hair Straighter

10. Popcorn & Cola

11. Shaving Brush & Shaving Gel

12. Burger & Fries

13. Shoes & Socks

14. Shampoo & Body Wash Gel

15. Detergent Liquid & Fabric Softener

Cross-selling is ubiquitous in almost every product segment. Banks sell credit cards, insurance, securities trading accounts, etc., to customers with a savings bank account. On online shopping portals, cross-selling is all-pervasive. Consider this: on shopping portals, while checking out, the shopper is given options to buy products that others have bought or add ancillary products to avail free shipping. Most of the time, the shopper adds a previously purchased product to avail free shipping. When most customers are about to pay for their purchases, they are more likely to make an impulse purchase given the reasonable offer.

Consider fast-food chains that offer fries or cola in addition to the burger or suggest a meal that includes all three. Multiplex cinema chains have also mastered this strategy, suggesting  the purchase of a tub of popcorn along with the movie tickets, which will be served at their seats during the movie— and one falls for it effortlessly.

Below are some of the ways by which cross-selling can be accomplished:

- Discounts on a related product on purchase of an existing product

- Combo packs which include multiple complementary products

- Introductory pack of a new supplementary product at an attractive discount along with the existing product

- Offer cashback or rewards points on the purchase of complementary products

- Sending reminders to shoppers who have abandoned their cart to continue shopping with additional products at a discount
  (Existing product means products that are already in the shopping cart of the customer)

The advantages of cross-selling are as follows:

- Shoppers get the option to quickly add products that complement the ones which are already in their cart

- Opportunity for the marketers to showcase the width of their catalog to the consumers

- Increases the average order value (AOV) of the customers

- Makes customers prepone their purchase for ancillary products, and this ensures that they do not visit a competing store to buy such products

- Increases customer loyalty and retention as consumers expect the marketer to launch new products at a regular frequency and offer attractive discounts on them

Cross-selling efforts have to be undertaken based on data analysis to target customers who have shown some flexibility in buying cross-sold products. Data mining should be performed to understand when, how, and how much of the additional product the shopper is likely to buy. Some of these parameters may be as follows:

a. When is the customer most likely to consider buying additional products, i.e., while reviewing the cart or checking out?

b. When does the customer prefer to buy additional products, i.e., when offered a discount or a cashback?

c. Which are the categories of products with which additional products are bought by the customer?

d. What is the average price of additional products being bought by the customers?

## 6.2 Up-Selling

Up-selling means getting customers to spend more by selling a premium or upgraded version of the product that they intend to buy. Upselling primarily involves selling more profitable products than the ones that customers plan to buy. It also includes selling top-ups to the base version of the product. The idea here is to increase the AOV of the customers before they make their final purchases. Up-selling is beneficial to consumers as well because they derive more value from the upgraded product. Generally, consumers don't mind buying a new and upgraded product if it eliminates the shortcomings of the existing one or when the differential cost of acquiring the new product is affordable.

Upselling can also involve selling add-ons or extensions to increase the functionality or life span of a product until an upgraded version is launched.

**Some of the examples of Up-selling, which include making the consumers upgrade to a higher version of a product or service offering, are as follows:**

|     | To | From |
| --- | --- | --- |
| 1. | Split AC | Window AC |
| 2. | Premium variant of a car | Standard version |
| 3. | Four blades razor | Three blades |
| 4. | 5G mobile phone | 4G mobile phone |
| 5. | First-class airline seat | Economy seat |
| 6. | A full version of a software | Basic version |
| 7. | Wireless printer | Wired printer |
| 8. | Anti-glare spectacle glasses | Standard glasses |
| 9. | High Definition (HD) cable TV service | Standard Definition (SD) |
| 10. | Premium subscription | Standard subscription |
| 11. | Full body health check-up package | Single parameter test |
| 12. | Faster delivery courier service | Standard delivery |
| 13. | The latest version of a gaming console | Older version |
| 14. | Premium scratch resistant paint | Standard quality |
| 15. | Laptop with latest processor | Older version processor |

Let us understand why companies prefer Up-Selling:

- To shift customers to the next generation technology, which offers a better user experience, before the competitors start targeting the same customers

- To gradually phase out older versions of products which may not be economical to produce

- To make more profits on new products priced at a premium during the introduction or launch stage

- To phase out old products which have reached their maturity stage and thus have declining economies of scale

- When an organization plans to cease the servicing of an existing version beyond a certain point, especially for consumer-durable products

- For faster market penetration of the upgraded product to get more economies of scale

- Acquiring new customers is relatively more expensive than up-selling to existing ones

The advantages of Up-Selling to the existing customer base are as follows:

- Faster rollout of new products to further spur the market penetration

- Quick customer conversions to upgraded products at the least cost

- Selling to existing customers is less expensive than selling to a new set of target audiences

- Shorten the time needed to completely phase out the old version to free up resources for a new version

- Customers are delighted to get a better solution to their needs

- Increase average cart value and profitability as new versions are priced higher at a premium

**The DOs and DONTs of Up-Selling are as follows:**

**DOs**

- Identify customers' pain points with the existing product and explain how the upgraded product will fix those shortcomings.

- Explain feature-to-feature comparison of old and new versions so that the customer can appreciate the value of the premium version.

- Offer a special time-bound discount to enable the customers to make an early decision.

- Promote the products with high user ratings and display the ratings at the point of sale.

- Give better display and visibility for the products with testimonials from users.

- Offer good value combo packs containing the new product to aid decision making especially for impulse purchase products.

- Let customers choose the top-up of their liking from the menu of options available.

- Offer a product that can reduce customers' recurring expenses, time, and efforts involved in using the product.

- Promote products that are environmentally and health-friendly as consumers are ready to pay a premium for such products.

**DO NOTs**

- Do not recommend an upgrade that is significantly more expensive than the older version. More than a 25 percent price difference may not work.

- Do not be too aggressive; otherwise, the customer may get apprehensive.

- Do not give too many options of up-sold products which makes it difficult and complex for the customer to decide whether to buy the product.

- Do not make them feel that they are making the wrong choice by not upgrading.

# 6.3 Value-Added Selling

The term 'value-added' means adding more economic value to products before selling them to consumers. Value-added selling enhances product offering by constantly delivering more value to delight the customers without spending extra money. It means building a strong value proposition for the products so that consumers continue their association with the company. Value-added strategy implies that a company increases the derived value of its products for the consumers.

In today's hyper-competitive market place where market shares have shrunk over time, brands must stay relevant for the consumers. In many product categories, the line of differentiation between brands has almost blurred. This has led to the commoditization of many products and services. The price of the product has become the only deciding factor for most of the consumers' purchase decisions. Companies have to constantly strive to enhance the cost-benefit-value proposition to retain customer loyalty in such a scenario. Adding value to products and services is very important as it provides consumers with an incentive to continue making purchases, thus increasing a company's sales revenue.

## Examples of Value-Added Selling

- Mobile telecom services company giving discount coupons for restaurants and movie tickets to its subscribers

- Banks offer free door-step banking to their premium bank account holders

- Digital payment apps give cash back to their customers on utility bill payments

- Free access to the VIP lounge at an airport for premium credit card holders

- Giving free annual maintenance service to customers buying consumer durables

- E-commerce websites are giving special discounts, free and faster shipping to their customers who are their membership plan holders

- Companies are offering an extended warranty or free servicing for consumer appliances, electronic devices, automobiles

- Airlines give their fliers free upgrades to a higher class if seats are available

- Bundling free gaming discs along with game consoles

- Offering coupons of various brands on a yearly subscription to a news portal

- Offering complimentary car upholstery while selling a car

The characteristics of Value-Added Selling are illustrated in Figure 6.2.

**Figure 6.2** **Characteristics of Value-Added Selling**

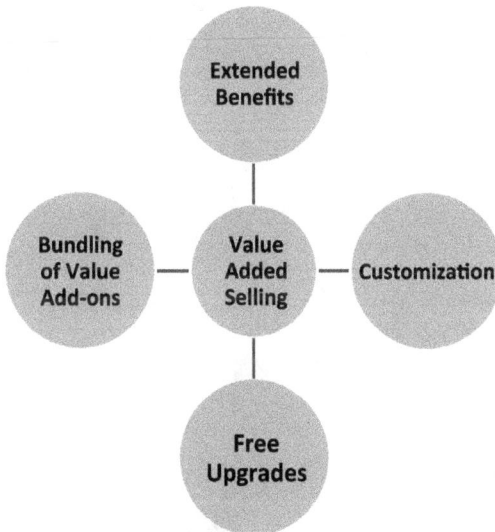

**Why should companies do value-added selling?**

- To ensure consumer loyalty and delight by enhancing the value proposition for the consumers

- To create an entry barrier for the competition

- To create differentiation from the competitor's product

- To create a Unique Selling Proposition for their products or services

However, value-added selling has to be a permanent feature rather than offering occasional discounts. Consumers now have access to a varied range of products and services at their disposal. As a result, companies have to constantly strive to create a competitive advantage for themselves.

# Chapter Summary

◆ Cross-Selling, Up-Selling, and Value Added selling techniques are widely used by companies to increase their sales revenue.

◆ Companies have to constantly build an enhanced value proposition for their customers, which can be delivered using these techniques.

◆ Understanding how and when to use these techniques is crucial for delivering a delightful experience to the customers.

# Quiz 6

1. Cross-Selling is used to persuade customers to buy a product which is _____ to the product they intend to buy.

   a. complementary

   b. ancillary

   c. supplementary

   d. all of the above

2. Following is an example of Cross-Selling:

   a. Pen-drive and optical Mouse

   b. Spectacles and contact lenses

   c. Both A & B

   d. None of the above

3. Up-selling means getting customers to spend more by selling_____.

   a. upgraded version of a product

   b. top-ups over the base version of a product

   c. multiple units of the same product

   d. options A & B

4. **Fast food chains persuade someone to buy fries or cola with the burger. This is an example of _____.**

   a. cross-selling

   b. up-selling

   c. value-added selling

   d. options A & B

5. **Creating a pleasant in-store ambiance can make consumers buy _____.**

   a. complementary products

   b. products they do not intend to buy

   c. impulse purchase products

   d. options A & C

6. **Selling complementary products has the following advantage _____**

   a. It increases the average cart value of the customers

   b. It makes customers prepone their purchases

   c. It is an opportunity to showcase the entire catalog to customers

   d. All of the above

**7. Which of the following is an example of Up-Selling?**

   a. Selling PlayStation 5 instead of PlayStation 4

   b. Selling a red color car instead of blue color

   c. Selling a sanitizer along with a face mask during a
      pandemic

   d. All of the above

**8. Which of the following comes under Value-Added Selling?**

   a. Giving discount coupons of a supermarket store to the
      customer who buys a television

   b. Bundling free extra blades along with a shaving razor

   c. Options A & B

   d. None of the above

**9. A cinema hall offers two free tickets to its patrons for every
   24 tickets they buy in a year. This is called_____**

   a. up-selling

   b. cross-selling

   c. value-added selling

   d. options A&B

10. A company gives a free helicopter ride to customers who buy a holiday package. This comes under___

   a. up-selling

   b. value-added selling

   c. both A & B

   d. none of the above

| Answers | 1 – d | 2 – c | 3 – d | 4 – a | 5 – c |
|---------|-------|-------|-------|-------|-------|
|         | 6 – d | 7 – a | 8 – c | 9 – c | 10 – b |

# CASE STUDY:
# Analyzing Cross-Selling Trends

A well-known youth brand that sells various accessories like watches, bags, eyewear, wallets, perfumes, and face masks wants to do secondary research to identify the industry-wide cross-selling trend for the category of its products.

Its marketing team browsed three leading online shopping portals which sell the same products and identified 100 pairs of products that were suggested, across these portals, for cross-selling to the consumers. Accordingly, the data for 100 pairs was plotted as given in Table 6.1. The primary product was represented on one axis and the suggested cross-selling product on the other. Analysis of this data helped them understand the trend in cross-selling of these products.

**Table 6.1**    **Data for cross-selling suggestions**

| | Primary Product | | | | | | |
|---|---|---|---|---|---|---|---|
| | Watch | Bag | Eye wear | Wallet | Perfume | Face Mask | Total |
| Cross-Selling Product | Number of pairs | | | | | | |
| Watch | - | 3 | 4 | 6 | 2 | 2 | **17** |
| Bag | 2 | - | 4 | 3 | 3 | 4 | **16** |
| Eyewear | 3 | 2 | - | 4 | 1 | 6 | **16** |
| Wallet | 6 | 4 | 3 | | 2 | 3 | **18** |
| Perfume | - | 3 | 3 | 6 | - | 3 | **15** |
| Face Mask | 3 | 2 | 5 | 5 | 3 | - | **18** |
| | | | | | | | **100** |

Analysis of the data given in Table 6.1 gives the total number of times a pair of products was suggested for cross –selling as follows:

| | |
|---|---|
| **Watch & Bag** | 2 + 3 = 5 |
| **Watch & Eyewear** | 3 + 4 = 7 |
| **Watch & Wallet** | 6 + 6 = 12 |
| **Watch & Perfume** | 0 + 2 = 2 |
| **Watch & Facemask** | 3 + 2 = 5 |
| **Bag & Eye Wear** | 2 + 4 = 6 |
| **Bag & Perfume** | 3 + 3 = 6 |
| **Bag & Wallet** | 4 + 3 = 7 |
| **Bag & Facemask** | 2 + 4 = 6 |
| **Eyewear & Wallet** | 3 + 4 = 7 |
| **Eyewear & Perfume** | 3 + 1 = 4 |
| **Eyewear & Facemask** | 5 + 6 = 11 |
| **Wallet & Perfume** | 6 + 2 = 8 |
| **Wallet & Facemask** | 5 +3 = 8 |
| **Perfume & Facemask** | 3 + 3 = 6 |

As per the above analysis, Watch & Wallet as a cross-selling pair is the most (12 times) suggested one, whereas Watch & Perfume is the least (2 times) suggested one.

# Off-Class Assignment:
# Analyzing Cross-Selling Trends

Make groups of 3 students each. Each group can be asked to do similar research for any two other industry verticals.

# Chapter 7

# Channel Conflict: Reasons to Resolution

As we have understood in the previous chapters, companies sell their products and services through a chain of channel partners or sales intermediaries known as distributors, wholesalers, retailers, and agents. They form an integral part of the supply chain by connecting marketers to the last mile, i.e., consumers. There is interdependence among the intermediaries and the marketer to ensure that the products reach the last stage of the supply chain. In order to ensure that the supply chain works seamlessly, all concerned have to follow specific guidelines, rules, objectives, policies, and terms of trade specified either by the marketer or the intermediaries. However, there might be instances when there is a deviation from these norms, leading to a channel conflict. In this chapter, we will explore this aspect of channel dynamics.

Key learnings for the reader from this chapter include the reader's understanding of the following:

- What is meant by channel conflict among the intermediaries?

- Types of channel conflicts

- Reasons and consequences of channel conflict

- Styles and techniques to effectively resolve channel conflict

# 7.1 Channel Conflict

Channel conflict can be described as a 'Situation of discord or disagreement between members of the same sales channel system.'

Channel conflict occurs when the operations of one or more entities of the sales channel affect the business prospects, sales, profitability, market share, vision, or objectives of any other channel partner.

Every organization has to plan its distribution channel to ensure maximum market penetration for its products and customer satisfaction while achieving growth and profitability. However, there can be instances when the business operations do not function as per the plan due to channel conflict among the trading partners. This channel conflict can be varied, and the conflict has to be resolved to streamline the business operations.

# 7.2 Causes of Channel Conflict

1. **Territory clash by channel partners**

This is one of the main reasons for channel conflict where one of the sales channel partners supplies products in the territory assigned to another intermediary. Companies or brands usually appoint sales channel intermediaries exclusively for each territory or market area to sell their products. These intermediaries further sell to the next level of channel partners in their respective territories. At times a situation may arise when one or more channel partners sell the products outside the territory assigned to them.

For example, Company A has appointed intermediary 'X' to sell its products in the USA and intermediary 'Y 'for European markets on a sole and exclusive basis. However, X sells products in Europe also to gain more sales or for any other reason. This affects the sales potential of Y while reducing the sales and profitability of Y. This is called Territory Clash / Encroachment by X. In such a case, Company A has to intervene and resolve this conflict after understanding the challenges and reasons which led to this situation. Some of the reasons for this situation can be as follows:

    a. X is not able to achieve the target set by Company A, and hence it sells products in the territory of Y to meet the target.

    b. Y may have sold products in the territory of X earlier. Hence X is selling in Y's territory as a retaliatory action.

    c. There could be animosity between X and Y due to some personal or professional reasons; hence X is encroaching upon Y's territory.

In this case, Company A has the following recourse:

i.  To take appropriate measures so that X meets its target.

ii. To rationalize the targets set for X.

iii. To appoint new intermediaries in place of either X or Y or both.

iv. To get the issue resolved amicably between X and Y.

## 2. High targets are given to channel intermediary

If one of the channel intermediaries sets a very high target for another intermediary that does not match the market's demand potential, there could be a conflict between the intermediaries regarding target rationalization. The situation will thus have to be reviewed and efforts taken to resolve the conflict.

## 3. Inefficiencies at the intermediary's end

An the intermediary may not able to meet its targets due to inefficiencies at its end. These inefficiencies could be related to sales force management, inefficient market coverage efforts, inventory management, operational issues. Hence, there is a conflict between the marketer and the intermediary as the sales targets are not met. This situation will thus have to be reviewed to remove the inefficiencies, or a new intermediary will have to be appointed.

## 4. Multiple channel partners for the same territory

If there are multiple channel partners appointed for the same territory by the marketer, then there can be a situation where the channel partners start selling products to the same set of customers by offering lower prices than that offered by others to achieve their respective sales targets. This can result in a price war between them. In turn, this reduces the return on investment on the marketer's products for the intermediary. The marketer will thus have to increase the profit margin given to the intermediaries, or rationalize the sales targets, or take steps to increase the market size for its products, so that all intermediaries get sufficient sales volumes and return on their investment. Otherwise, the intermediaries may divert their resources to competitors' products or other business ventures. This can affect the sales and image of the marketer.

## 5. Discriminatory terms of trade

Channel conflict can arise if the marketer offers different terms of business to different channel intermediaries. The intermediaries who get better terms of trade from the marketer can offer favorable terms of trade to the same set of customers compared to what other intermediaries can offer. The conflict here is in disharmony among the channel partners, resulting in the channel intermediaries moving out.

## 6. Role Ambiguity

At times there can be a situation wherein the role and responsibilities of the distributor are not outlined properly by the marketer, which can affect the achievement of sales objectives and thus result in channel conflict between them.

## Example
i.  The marketer expects the intermediary to assume more responsibility for market penetration; however, the

intermediary essentially functions as an order fulfillment agency.

## 7. Key Accounts Management Policy

Marketers often prefer to sell their products directly to large customer accounts rather than route the orders through intermediaries. Hence there can be disharmony between them as the intermediary may not be motivated enough to achieve the sales targets by focusing only on smaller customer accounts.

### Example

i.  Many FMCG brands prefer to sell products directly to supermarket chains because they get orders in large volumes from these chains. Also, the brands perform many joint sales promotional activities with these chain stores and hence prefer to sell the goods directly to them. However, this results in conflict with the intermediaries, who do not get an opportunity to sell products to large key accounts.

## 8. Inventory management challenges

Intermediaries may face the following challenges with regards to inventory management:

i.  Persuasion by the marketer to maintain higher inventory levels than the usual demand of the products increases the working capital requirement of the intermediary and thus reduces its Return on Investment (ROI).

ii. Unsold inventory that the marketer is not ready to accept as returns nor supports the intermediary in any manner to sell the goods further in the channel. This results in disharmony between them as the intermediary will suffer losses due to unsold inventory.

iii. The marketer pushes sales of slow-moving SKUs along with fast-moving SKUs to the intermediary to achieve the sales targets. The slow-moving SKUs block the working capital of the intermediary or remain unsold, which results in a loss for the intermediary.

iv. During a new product launch, marketers set very high sales targets and aggressively push sales to the intermediaries. The intermediaries thus feel pressured to maintain a high inventory level which can block their working capital for an extended time frame. It can also result in unsold inventory if the sales volumes of the product are not as expected.

9. **Clash of Interest**

There can be a conflict of interest between the marketer and the intermediaries due to the following reasons:

i. If the intermediaries start dealing in products of the marketer's competitors despite the terms of business restricting them from doing so, it will result in a breach of the terms of contract and a conflict of interest.

ii. The intermediary launches a brand which competes with the marketer's brand. Such brands are called 'Dealer Brands.'

**Example**

i. An outsourced bottling agency of a beverage manufacturer launches its own brand of the same beverage, which leads to a breach of the terms of contract.

10. **Payment delays by the intermediary**

There can be delays in releasing the payments of the marketer by an intermediary (distributor) due to the following reasons:

i. Payment delays from other intermediaries (retailers) which are serviced by the said intermediary (distributor)

ii. Inefficient financial management by the intermediary resulting in delayed payments to the marketer

iii. The intermediary is stuck with unsold inventory or has faced bad debts from other intermediaries, thus extending the overall payment cycle

The above situations can result in a conflict between the marketer and the intermediary due to payment-related issues.

## 7.3 Types of Channel Conflict

Types of channel conflict can be classified as illustrated in Figure 7.1.

**Figure 7.1** **Types of Channel Conflict**

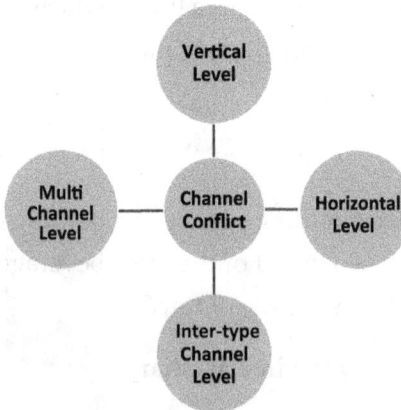

**Source:** https://theinvestorsbook.com/channel-conflict.html by Prachi M, The Investors Book, July 27, 2019

## Vertical Level

In a vertical level conflict, a higher-level channel partner has a conflict with a lower-level channel partner or vice-versa. For example:

a. Channel conflict between distributors and retailers regarding the level of profit margin offered for the products

b. Distributors start dealing in products of the marketer's competitors despite not being allowed to do so as per their business terms, thus resulting in a conflict of interest

## Horizontal Level

Conflict among the channel partners belonging to the same level.

*E.g.* Conflict between two distributors of different regions regarding territory encroachment

## Inter-type

Conflict is due to the channel partner's diversification into products of a different category than the marketer's.

*E.g.* A retailer who has been given an exclusive franchisee to sell a marketer's products starts selling products of other categories from the same premises, thus diluting the focus on selling the marketer's products.

## Multi-Channel Level

When the marketer sells products through multiple channels, there is a conflict between the channel partners.

E.g., A marketer has appointed Distributor 'A' to sell products to large format supermarket chains and Distributor 'B' for selling to smaller stand-alone retail stores. Nevertheless, Distributor 'B' sells products to large format stores as well to get more sales. Hence Distributor 'A' will be in conflict with Distributor 'B.'

# 7.4 Consequences of Channel Conflict

Consequences of channel conflict are as follows (see Figure 7.2).

a. **Price Battles:** There can be a price war among the intermediaries to gain more market share due to channel conflict. This may eventually affect the profitability of the intermediaries or Return on Investment (ROI) on the marketer's products. Hence, existing or new channel partners may not be motivated to deal in marketer's products.

b. **Sales Revenue Decreases:** Channel conflict may disturb the supply chain of products till the conflict is resolved, and hence the sales revenue declines in the interim period.

c. **Customer Dissatisfaction:** Channel conflict can lead to customer dissatisfaction if the stock availability of the marketer's products is affected due to differences between the intermediaries who may not be interested in selling the marketer's products.

d. **Exit of Intermediary:** For the marketer, it is imperative to retain the intermediaries for stable business operations. However, in case of a significant channel conflict, there is a possibility that the intermediaries may exit the channel.

e. **Affects Brand Image:** Unsatisfied and demotivated intermediaries do not carry a good brand image of the marketer. This can affect the marketer's current and future business prospects.

| Figure 7.2 | **Consequences of Channel Conflict** |

## 7.5 Conflict Resolution Tools

Following are some of the ways or tools to practically manage channel conflict situations (see Figure 7.3).

### Mediation, Arbitration, and Diplomacy

**Mediation:** Seeking the intervention of a third party to resolve the conflict amicably.

**Arbitration:** To appoint an arbitrator who suggests a resolution after allowing both sides to present their respective case.

**Diplomacy:** Representatives of both parties review the conflict situation and find a solution which is a win-win proposition for both sides.

### Co-optation

The manufacturer should hire an expert who has already gained experience in managing channel conflicts in other organizations, as a member of the grievance redressal committee or board of directors for addressing such conflicts.

### Dealer Councils and Trade Associations

Every industry segment typically has Dealer Councils or Trade Associations who can take a neutral and unbiased view of the conflict situation and accordingly devise specific guidelines which apply to all the members of these bodies. They can also mediate between the aggrieved parties to end the conflict.

### Legal Action

When the conflict is critical and cannot be resolved through dialogue, the parties can seek legal remedy in the court of law.

| Figure 7.3 | Conflict Resolution Tools |

## 7.6 Conflict Management Styles

Whenever there is a conflict situation, it can be managed in different styles with different outcomes. Figure 7.4 illustrates these styles and their respective outcomes.

| Figure 7.4 | **Conflict Management Styles** |

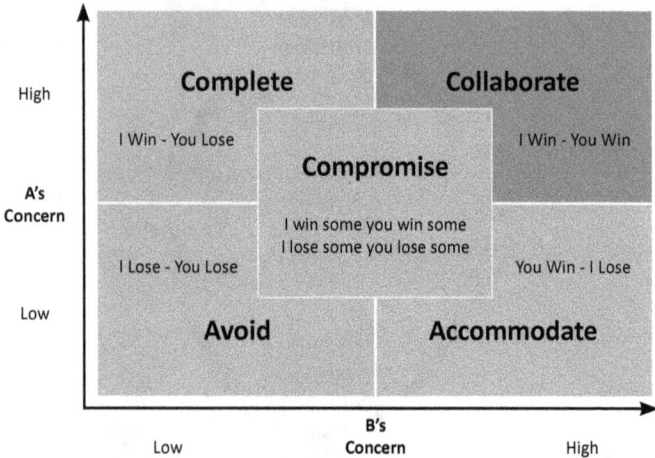

**Source:** Thomas-Kilmann Conflict Mode Instrument (TKI), https://kilmanndiagnostics.com/overview-thomas-kilmann-conflict-mode-instrument-tki/

## Avoid

In this situation, both A's and B's concerns are of low importance, so they avoid resolving the conflict. Nevertheless, the conflict persists and can resurface in the future as a matter of more significant concern.

It is an I lose – You lose outcome

i.e., A loses – B loses outcome

## Compete

In this situation, A's concern is greater than that of B. Hence, A shows signs of competition and aggression to reign over B. However, it is a one-sided victory for A, which may not last long as B's concern has not been resolved.

It is an I win – You lose outcome

i.e., A wins – B loses outcome

## Accommodate

Here B's concern is of a higher degree than that of A. Thus A accommodates and resolves B's concern without addressing its own concern. However, it is a one-sided victory for B, which may not last long as A's concern has not been resolved.

It is a You win – I lose outcome

i.e., B wins – A loses outcome

## Collaborate

A & B collaborate to address their concerns, both of which are higher-order to create a win-win situation.

It is an I win – You win outcome; i.e., A wins – B wins' outcome

## Compromise

This is an ideal outcome wherein both A & B collaborate to find an outcome that involves a compromise formula. Both A & B reach common ground by resolving certain aspects of their respective concerns. At the same time, both compromise on specific aspects of their respective concerns in the more significant interest of a success formula.

It is an I win some – You win some & I lose some – You lose some outcome

i.e., A wins some – B wins some & A loses some – B loses some outcome

Conflict Management styles can also be represented in terms of the efforts required to handle the situation and expected results. (See Figure 7.5)

**Figure 7.5** **Conflict Management Styles**

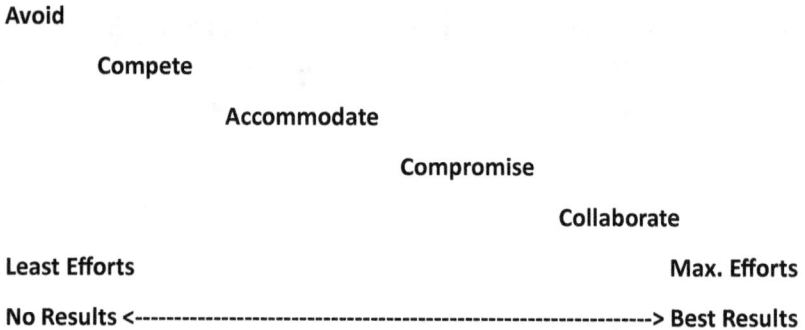

**Avoid**

       **Compete**

          **Accommodate**

              **Compromise**

                   **Collaborate**

**Least Efforts**                                         **Max. Efforts**

**No Results <-------------------------------------------------------------------> Best Results**

Source: Adapted from The Thomas-Kilmann Conflict Mode Instrument (TKI).

As per the above representation, the Avoidance style requires the least effort but yields no results, and the conflict remains in abeyance and resurfaces later on. On the other hand, the Collaboration style requires maximum efforts and yields the best results to address the concerns of both parties.

# Chapter Summary

◆ Channel conflict is an issue in sales management with many types, dimensions, causes, consequences, and resolution techniques and approaches.

◆ Channel conflict can have severe consequences for an organization's business operations if a resolution is not achieved in a timely and effective manner.

◆ The best way to resolve any channel conflict depends on how critical the conflict is and the result or outcome expected from the resolution.

# Quiz 7

1. **Which of the following is a cause of channel conflict?**

   a. Territory clash by intermediaries

   b. Multiple channel partners for the same market area

   c. Role ambiguity between intermediaries

   d. All of the above

2. **Which of the following is not a style of conflict management?**

   a. Avoidance

   b. Compete

   c. Continue

   d. Compromise

3. **Which of the following is not a cause of channel conflict?**

   a. Inefficient inventory management

   b. Inefficient market coverage

   c. Conflict of interest

   d. None of the above

4. In a vertical level conflict_____.

   a. higher-level channel intermediary has a conflict with a lower level one

   b. lower-level channel intermediary has a conflict with a higher level one

   c. both A & B

   d. none of the above

5. **Which of the following is true for horizontal level conflict?**

   a. Conflict is among channel partners belonging to the same level

   b. Higher-level intermediary has a conflict with a lower level one

   c. Role ambiguity between intermediaries

   d. All of the above

6. **Which of the following is not a cause of payment delay by an intermediary?**

   a. Inefficient financial management

   b. Unsold inventory

   c. Low inventory level

   d. Bad debts

7. **Conflict due to channel partner's diversification into products of different categories than that of the marketer's products is which level of conflict?**

    a. Horizontal

    b. Inter-type

    c. Vertical

    d. Multi-channel

8. **When the marketer sells products through various channels in the same market, it is called a _____ conflict.**

    a. horizontal

    b. multi-channel

    c. inter-type

    d. none of the above

9. **Which of the following is not a consequence of a channel conflict?**

    a. Exit of intermediary

    b. Price war

    c. Price alignment

    d. None of the above

**10.** Which of the following is a measure for conflict resolution?

   a.  Mediation

   b.  Arbitration

   c.  Co-optation

   d.  All of the above

| **Answers** | 1 – d | 2 – c | 3 – d | 4 – c | 5 – a |
|-------------|-------|-------|-------|-------|-------|
|             | 6 – c | 7 – b | 8 – b | 9 – c | 10 – d |

# Role Play Activity

Select a few students from the class and assign them their roles of an intermediary or a marketer as per a conflict situation assigned to them. They have to manage the conflict by using conflict management or resolution techniques discussed in this chapter. After the role-play, ask the class to comment on the interaction between the students in the role play and also share their feedback on the conflict management approach adopted by them. The following conflict situations can be given for the role play:

1. An intermediary, the sole and exclusive distributor of a marketer's products for a particular territory, has started dealing in products of the latter's competitor. This has resulted in a conflict of interest between them (Student No.1 and No.2 act as the intermediary and marketer, respectively).

2. A distributor of a marketer who sells licensed merchandise of an animated series has started selling unlicensed products of the same series. This conflict is of great concern for the marketer of the original merchandise (Student No.1 and No.2 act as the distributor and marketer, respectively).

3. A wholesaler of a leading lubricant brand has started selling the marketer's products to the customers of another wholesaler at a meager price to gain additional market share. This has led to a horizontal conflict between both the wholesalers (Student No.1 & No.2 act as the intermediaries and Student No.3 as the marketer).

# Case Discussion:
# Dealer Brands - Conflict of Interest

A marketer's distributor plans to launch its own 'Dealer Brand,' which can compete with the marketer's brand. Hence there is a conflict of interest between them. Which type of conflict management technique would be an ideal solution for resolving this conflict?

## Suggested Answer

Adopting the collaboration technique of conflict management could be an ideal solution where the marketer and the intermediary can jointly launch, market, and sell the new product in the market. This way, they can instead turn the conflict into a business opportunity. They can pursue the following sales strategy:-

a. Launch the new brand for a target market different from the existing market for the marketer's brand. This will ensure that both the brands co-exist without cannibalizing each other's sales revenue.

b. The marketer can take the responsibility of Pull Sales by creating awareness and recall for the new brand through consumer-oriented promotional activities.

c. The distributor can manage Push Sales of the new brand by selling the products in its existing distribution chain.

d. The distributor can also leverage the marketer's distribution network to sell the new brand in other markets where the distributor does not have an established network.

Thus, both parties can leverage the synergies and create a win-win proposition to manage the conflict without affecting their existing business relationship and sales revenues. This way, both parties can expand their business by diversifying in new markets with a new brand.

# CASE STUDY:
# Producer-multiplex revenue sharing talks failed[6]

A Bollywood film producers' and multiplex owners' meeting on Tuesday ended in a deadlock over revenue sharing row. According to industry insiders, the two parties failed to reach a mutual understanding over the rationalization of revenue sharing of films. The issue started in February when producers demanded a 50 percent revenue share for all films. The multiplexes refused the demand but, in later talks, agreed to give 50, 40, and 30 percent revenue share during subsequent weeks after the release week.

The United Producers and Distributors Forum (UPDF) declared in early March not to push any new film in multiplexes from April 4 onwards. "The talks have stalled as multiplex owners are not willing to come up with more than the 50-40-30 ratio and are rigid on their stand. We are now formalizing a plan to release all new films in single screens and independent multiplexes across the country," Muktesh Bhatt, the spokesperson for UPDF, told IANS over the phone from Mumbai. "We will even come out with the plan in the next 15 days", he added. An industry insider, who was present at the meeting, said, "Multiplexes are not willing to budge. Despite that, we (producers-distributors) are willing to come down from 50 percent. They (multiplex owner) said the 50-40-30 weekly ratio is the best they can do and didn't come up with any other solution. We are now not going to reschedule any meets," said the insider, pleading anonymity. Production houses like UTV Motion Pictures, which also has a distribution arm,

---

6. Excerpts from https://www.indiatoday.in/latest-headlines/story/producer-multiplex-revenue-sharing-talks-failed-46620-2009-05-05

have decided to release their forthcoming films like "Kaminay," "Kisan," and "Main Aur Mrs. Khanna" in single-screen theaters. "Since there is no resolution on the national chains of multiplex issue, UTV will proceed to start releasing its big and small movies in single screen theatres and non-national chain multiplexes nationwide from July onwards," Siddharth Roy Kapur, CEO UTV Motion Pictures, said in a statement. A precursor was laid to the Tuesday meeting on April 29 when talks between the producers and multiplex owners ended on a "no result but positive" note.

Study the above case and identify the cause, types, and consequences of the channel conflict between the multiplexes and producers. Also, comment on the conflict resolution technique used to manage the conflict situation.

## Solution

The types of channel conflicts in the case study are as follows:

The multiplexes are the intermediaries of producers and distributors of films.

1.  The cause of channel conflict was revenue sharing arrangement or trade terms between the multiplexes and the film producers, who can be considered as retailers and marketers, respectively, in the film exhibition business. The producers were asking for a share of 50% of the ticket sales revenue for all films. However, the multiplexes were not ready to do so.

2.  The type of channel conflict was 'Vertical Conflict,' i.e., between the intermediaries of the same sales channel.

3.  The consequence of the conflict was the temporary exit of

intermediaries from the sales channel as they refused to screen the movies for almost a month. The producers, too, decided to release their films only in single-screen theaters.

4. The conflict management techniques used were:

   a. Mediation by Trade Association as a third party was explored. However, the multiplexes adopted an aggressive approach to channel conflict resolution by refusing to accept the producers' demand.

   b. Diplomacy technique and compromise approach were used to resolve the conflict as both the parties re-negotiated revenue-sharing terms to 50%, 40% and 30% share for subsequent weeks.

*This page is intentionally left blank*

# Chapter 8

## Managing Key Accounts

M any marketers prefer to deal directly with customers who regularly order goods or services in large volumes rather than engaging intermediaries. The said customers are referred to as Key Accounts because they give the marketer or the manufacturer substantial business. Supplying the goods directly to Key Accounts increases the profitability of the marketers as they do not have to give any trade margin/commission to the intermediaries. At the same time, the marketers can service these customers in a better manner than the intermediaries. Key Accounts also prefer to deal directly with the marketers to get lower prices, faster delivery of goods, and sales promotional support. Moreover, skipping an intermediary helps reduce the overall time taken to reach the end consumer.

Key learnings for the reader from this chapter include the reader's understanding of the following:

- How to manage Key Accounts effectively through best practices

- Which are the stages of Key Account Management (KAM)?

- What are the advantages and challenges of serving the Key Accounts directly?

## 8.1 Concept of Key Accounts Management

Research and Advisory Company Gartner describes Key Account Management (KAM) as: 'The process of planning and managing a mutually beneficial partnership between an organization and its most important customers. Key accounts are significant to an organization's sustainable, long-term growth and require a substantial investment of both time and resources. Salespeople must develop a clear strategy and program structure to serve and grow these strategic accounts'.

Key Account Management (KAM) builds and strengthens relationships with important clients. KAM, also called Strategic Account Management, plays a crucial role in achieving the organization's quantitative and qualitative objectives. KAM is required to nurture long-lasting relationships with the Key Accounts. KAM goes beyond the buyer-seller relationship, and it involves working together with the client's entire business team to find better ways of doing business. KAM helps the marketer deliver value that the clients are looking for rather than just selling products.

# 8.2 Managing Key Accounts Effectively

Key Accounts at times contribute a substantial share of a marketer's sales revenue. The famous 80:20 rule applies in this case, where 80% of sales come from 20% of strategic accounts. Hence it is essential to cater to these customers effectively by adopting the following best practices of KAM:

a. **Understand the profile of Key Accounts**

- Which markets or customer segments do they serve?

- What do their customers expect from them?

- What are their strategies and core competencies?

- How do they make money?

b. **Role of Key Accounts Manager**

The Key Account Manager who manages the Key Accounts at an organization has to build and nurture business relationships with his or her portfolio of key clients. KAM involves continuously providing them solutions to achieve their goals rather than just selling products to them. Key Account Management plays an essential role in B2B businesses where customization of the product offering plays an important role.

Thus, the key account manager has two responsibilities:

- Finalizing strategy to cater to the key accounts and ensuring it is implemented

- Developing relationships with Key Accounts to facilitate the implementation of the sales strategy

## c. Focus on most important customers

Organizations must have a clear understanding and guidelines on how to classify accounts as Key Accounts. Organizations should not consider customers as Key Accounts, just that they have been customers for a long time. Key Accounts are usually those customers who have the highest potential to sell the marketer's existing and new products to the end consumers and those who are loyal and consistent. This helps build significant value in the long term.

## d. Be a value provider and not a supplier

Key Accounts consider the marketer as a strategic partner and not as a supplier. Hence KAM requires flexibility to align with the customers' objectives while providing them with a suitable solution.

## e. Look for growth opportunities

KAM requires that the marketer is always looking to increase the sales revenue from existing Key Accounts and develop new key accounts. Key accounts can be provided with products which are exclusively packed for selling from their stores at discounted price. At the same time, special sales promotional activities should be done in collaboration with the key accounts to increase sales from their stores.

# 8.3 How to Choose Key Accounts

While choosing Key Accounts, the following check points should be considered:

i.  Consider only those clients who can order large volumes of products, e.g., a chain of supermarkets, education, and healthcare service providers, a retail chain selling consumer goods, or an industrial products company with multiple manufacturing units.

ii.  Is there a possibility of re-structuring the marketer's supply chain to provide enhanced and cost-efficient services to the clients? Or is the client ready to align its supply chain with that of the marketer for time and cost advantages?

iii.  Can the clients sell a high volume of new products of the marketer which can be introduced exclusively for them?

iv.  Is the client financially strong so that the marketer can take the risk of offering higher and extended credit lines?

v.  Can the client carry out joint consumer promotional activities with the marketer?

vi.  Does the client have the required automation and computerized systems and processes for ease of business?

vii.  Does the client have a footprint or presence across regions classified as a Key Account?

# 8.4 Stages of Key Accounts Management

Key Account Management (KAM) should progressively grow from a purely transactional relationship to a strategic partnership. The various stages of KAM are as follows (see Figure 8.1).

## 8.4.1 Transactional

The 'Key Account' here is just at the transactional stage because it is new. The marketer is just one of the multiple suppliers to the client. The relationship here thus assumes a transactional nature with pricing as the main criteria. The transactions at this stage are largely done through one person on both sides. The interactions are few, and demand forecasting can be done only for the short term. Some clients may remain at the transactional stage even after a long relationship if they do not consider vendors as partners in the long run.

## 8.4.2 Supportive

The 'key account' has now moved into a zone with more exchanges, driven by few people on both sides but still remaining at the transactional level. There is some amount of mutual understanding between both parties. If the 'key account' is of high potential, the marketer should review and evaluate the returns on its previous efforts for servicing the client and move forward accordingly.

## 8.4.3 Interdependent

At this stage, both parties are mutually dependent on each other. The marketer is one of the biggest suppliers to the Key Account. The exit of any one of them can lead to the loss of sizable business. The marketer will lose a significant account, thus denting its sales revenue. The Key Account will be affected too, as it will not have a supply of crucial products that it either sells further or uses as an input for manufacturing other products. At this stage, the client organization has also started considering the marketer as a crucial supplier of products for its future planning. The Key Account now is so critical and profitable for the marketer that it foresees the client as a critical entity for its sales forecast statistics.

## 8.4.4 Collaborative

This is the highest level of their relationship where both the parties have reached a collaborative and long-term strategy to leverage their core competencies and synergies for strategic purposes. For any stakeholders, the exit from here has many barriers and can have a far-reaching negative impact on their respective businesses. The communication between both entities is very transparent across the hierarchy.

**Figure 8.1**  **Stages of Key Account Management**

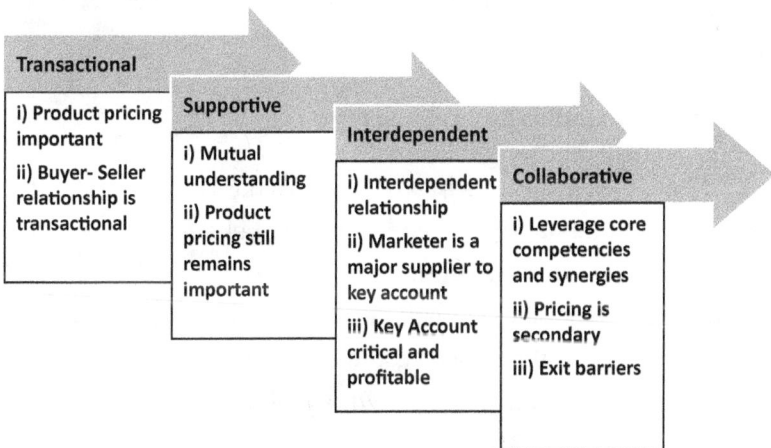

| Transactional | Supportive | Interdependent | Collaborative |
|---|---|---|---|
| i) Product pricing important | i) Mutual understanding | i) Interdependent relationship | i) Leverage core competencies and synergies |
| ii) Buyer- Seller relationship is transactional | ii) Product pricing still remains important | ii) Marketer is a major supplier to key account | ii) Pricing is secondary |
| | | iii) Key Account critical and profitable | iii) Exit barriers |

**Source:** Adapted from https://www.marketing91.com/key-account-management/

# 8.5 Advantages and Challenges of KAM

## 8.5.1 Advantages

### Increased profit margins

As the products/services are sold directly to the key accounts, the intermediaries are bypassed, leading to increased profit margins for the marketer. The marketer's return on investment also increases as there is faster rolling of the working capital employed in holding the inventory since intermediaries are not involved. The clients witness cost savings because they can source products in bulk at cheaper rates directly from the marketer.

### Shorter lead time

The products are shipped to the client's location directly from the marketer's warehouse, thus bypassing the intermediaries. This reduces the lead time needed for the products to be on retail shelves, thus decreasing the opportunity loss that can occur if the products are not available at the point of sale when consumers visit the store to shop.

### Insights on consumer buying behavior

KAM enables marketers to analyze sales data of the Key Accounts to understand consumers' buying behavior, tastes, preferences, and trends. Additionally, other data which is essential to analyze sales statistics and for forecasting demand is also available. It otherwise becomes difficult to source such relevant data from intermediaries who may not want to share such data. Moreover, if the intermediaries do not have adequate computerization for billing and inventory management systems, the relevant data to comprehend consumer buying behavior is not captured at the intermediary's end.

## Joint sales promotional activities

The marketer and key accounts can plan joint sales promotional activities across multiple points of sale at the Key Account stores.

## A strategic advantage over competitors

Building strong relationships with Key Accounts helps a marketer create entry barriers for the competitors, especially the new entrants. The new entrants may try to break the entry barriers by offering their products at lower rates to the key accounts than that offered by the established marketers. However, once the collaborative stage of KAM is reached, the pricing of products is not the central concern for both parties; it is instead about value discovery and delivery. This gives a strategic advantage to the marketers over its competitors.

## Learning from the experience curve

The practice of KAM leads to learning what works for large clients and what does not. What are they expecting: lower prices or value for their money? These learnings can be applied for managing other large accounts and defining best practices for KAM.

## 8.5.2 Challenges

i. Over-dependence on Key Accounts for large volume businesses can lead to neglecting the smaller client accounts, which cumulatively may have considerably more sales potential.

ii. There is a risk of the marketer's financial exposure being concentrated on few accounts rather than spread over several small accounts.

iii. Key Accounts negotiate hard for higher trade margins as they order products in large volumes for the entire region where they have a presence.

iv. Unlike traditional single-store outlets that are owner-driven, at key accounts, the buying of products is done by executives designated as merchandisers or buyers. In the case of a change of merchandising executive at a key account, there is a need to rebuild relations with the new executive. This may again take some time to get the relationship back to the earlier level.

v. Key Accounts are usually not flexible with their processes, systems, and policies. They want the marketers to align with their processes, which may lead to challenges for the marketer in managing the orders of the key accounts.

# Chapter Summary

◆ Key accounts may contribute a substantial proportion of the total sales of the marketer.

◆ KAM has various stages of progression from transactional to collaborative.

◆ Despite all the challenges, KAM is a crucial function for a marketer.

# Quiz 8

1. **A key account manager has the following responsibility_____.**

    a. building long-lasting relations with the key accounts

    b. ensuring promised value is delivered to the key accounts

    c. providing solutions rather than just selling products to the key accounts

    d. all of the above

2. **Which of the following is not a characteristic of KAM?**

    a. Acting as a partner to the critical account

    b. Being reactive rather than proactive

    c. Nurturing long-lasting relationships with the key accounts

    d. None of the above

3. **It is essential to understand which of the following aspects of a key account's profile?**

    a. The market or customer segment it caters to

    b. Its core competencies

    c. What customers of key accounts expect from them

    d. All of the above

**4. Which of the following is true with regards to KAM?**

   a. Appoint only clients who order in large quantities as key accounts

   b. Act as a partner to the key account

   c. Understand how do key accounts make their money

   d. All of the above

**5. Which of the following is not a stage of KAM?**

   a. Transactional

   b. Competitive

   c. Interdependent

   d. None of the above

**6. In the Transactional stage of KAM _____.**

   a. marketer is just one of the suppliers of the client

   b. competitive pricing is the main concern for the key account

   c. options A & B

   d. there is a lot of communication involved

7. **Which of the following is not true for the supportive stage of KAM?**

   a. There are more exchanges with the key account than in the transactional stage

   b. There is a mutual understanding between the marketer and key account

   c. The relationship with the key account moves beyond the pricing of products

   d. Options A & B

8. **In the Interdependent stage of KAM _____.**

   a. both the parties are mutually dependent on each other

   b. the marketer is one of the biggest suppliers of the Key Account

   c. exit of any one party can lead to a loss of sizeable sales revenue

   d. all of the above

9. **Which of the following is not true with regards to the collaborative stage of KAM?**

   a. Leveraging core competencies of both the parties

   b. Exploiting synergies for strategic purposes

   c. Pricing is the most important factor

   d. None of the above

10. Which of the following is true for the transactional stage of
    KAM?

    a. There are no exit barriers

    b. Exit barriers are powerful

    c. Pricing is not the main concern

    d. All of the above

| **Answers** | 1 – d | 2 – b | 3 – d | 4 – d | 5 – b |
|-------------|-------|-------|-------|-------|--------|
|             | 6 – c | 7 – c | 8 – d | 9 – c | 10 – a |

# CASE STUDY:
# Key Account Management - The Next Level

'Well Groomed' operates globally across North America, South America, Europe, Asia, and the Rest of the World (RoW). Well Groomed is a leading manufacturer of personal care products like eye liners, lipsticks, shampoos, face wash, hair conditioners, hair sprays, and nail paints, and is a top-five player globally. However, it has different rankings in each region that it has a presence. It is the strongest in North America.

Well Groomed's Key Accounts contribute about 60% of the total sales of the company. The company is a leading supplier of grooming products to one of the largest e-commerce portals called Myfashion.com, one of its key accounts. Myfashion.com is ranked number two among all online portals in North America. Well Groomed recently conducted a study to measure the profitability of each of its key accounts. This Key Account is significantly more profitable for Well-Groomed than an average key account. Well Groomed requires very few resources to cater to the demand of Myfashion.com. Their relationship is long-term and very positive. Their business has been stable for the past five years.

However, Myfashion.com's worldwide profit has been declining for the last two quarters. The reason for this is its high cost of operations. Hence, it has recently appointed a new CEO who wants all his business heads to reduce their cost of operations and pressure the suppliers to decrease the prices of their respective products sold to Myfashion.com. This will help the portal to increase its overall profitability. Accordingly, the new CEO has advised all its suppliers to reduce the prices of the products they sell to Myfashion.com.

The Key Account Manager at Well Groomed, who manages the key account of Myfashion.com, has enjoyed an excellent relationship with the business head of the grooming category of products at the latter. Both have now scheduled a meeting to discuss this matter.

## Question

How should Well Groomed manage this situation in terms of its Key Account Management?

## Suggested Answer

As evident from the case, Well Groomed and Myfashion.com are in the Interdependent stage of KAM. At this stage, both parties are mutually dependent on each other. Well Groomed is one of the biggest suppliers to Myfashion.com, which has started considering the former as a key supplier of products. Both enjoy a long-standing association. Myfashion account is now so critical and profitable for the marketer that it foresees the client as a key entity for its future planning.

The current situation is an excellent opportunity for both parties to elevate their relationship to the next level of KAM, i.e., the Collaborative Stage. Well Groomed should propose the following strategy to Myfashion.com so that the latter gets higher margins / or lower prices for the products the former supplies. At the same time, the profitability of Well Groomed should not be compromised.

- Both the parties should look at a more collaborative business proposition wherein they build a strategic relationship rather than just a buyer-seller relationship.

- Well Groomed can supply its existing products to Myfashion.com in an exclusive customized packaging specially designed for Myfashion.com.

- The packaging of these products can also carry the logo of Myfashion.com. This will help increase brand recall of Myfashion.com among its customers.

- Such products should be supplied to Myfashion.com at specially reduced prices subject to minimum order quantity and on a non-returnable basis.

- At the same time, few customized products can be jointly developed by both parties such that these products cater to specific requirements of Myfashion.com's customer base.

- Well Groomed can offer a revised target-based trade margin structure to Myfashion.com wherein the base margin offered to the latter is maintained at the current level, but additional incentive margins accrue to Myfashion.com as per the following structure:

  a. X % additional trade margin after it crosses an additional target of 15%.

  b. (X + Y) % additional trade margin on crossing an additional target of 20%.

This strategic model has advantages for both the parties as follows:

a. It ensures that Well Groomed does not have to increase the base margins it offers to Myfashion.com so that its current profitability is not compromised.

b. The additional incentive trade margin offered by Well-Groomed is payable only after Myfashion.com meets specific sourcing targets.

c. Well Groomed will get better brand visibility on Myfashion.com who will promote the exclusive packs on its website.

d. Myfashion.com will also increase profitability on Well Groomed's product range by sourcing particular incremental volume/value of products from Well Groomed.

e. Myfashion.com also gets specially developed and/or packaged products for its customers, which will increase its brand engagement with them.

The above model ensures that both parties increase their profitability compared to the current levels and increase their brand connection with the consumers.

*This page is intentionally left blank*

# Chapter 9

# Sales Promotions

Sales promotion is one of the most often-used tools to increase sales of any product or service. Many consumers have a perception that marketing and sales promotion are the same concepts. However, that is a misconception. Sales promotion is one part of the entire marketing process. It deals with incentivizing the consumer to buy the product, mostly with added gain. Sales promotions can have different objectives and expected outcomes and can be done through various methods. At the same time, it must be noted that it is different from advertising which is essentially a paid form of publicity. This chapter deals with the nuances of sales promotion in detail.

Key learnings for the reader from this chapter include the reader's understanding of the following:

- What is meant by sales promotion?

- Which are the sales promotions tools available to the marketer?

- Advantages and challenges of sales promotion

**According to ANA,** 'Promotion marketing includes tactics that encourage short-term purchase, influence trial and quantity of purchase, and are very measurable in volume, share, and profit.'[7]

"Sales promotion refers to those activities other than personal selling, advertising, and publicity that stimulate consumer purchasing and dealer effectiveness, such as – display shows and exhibitions, demonstrations, and various other non-recurrent selling efforts not in ordinary routine."[8]

Sales promotional activities can be broadly classified as follows:

     a. Consumer Promotions

     b. Trade Promotions

# 9.1 Consumer Promotions

Consumer promotions are targeted towards end consumers to induce or precipitate purchases of the marketer's products or services. To create mass promotion awareness, consumer promotion activities have to be ideally supported by advertising on mass media, online, and out-of-home media. Some of the consumer promotion activities are as follows (see Figure 9.1).

- Price–offs on products

- Combo packs at specially reduced prices

- BOGO (Buy 1, Get 1 free) offer

---

7. https://www.ana.net/content/show/id/baa-promotion-marketing

8. https://www.businessmanagementideas.com/sales-promotion-2/sales-promotion-objectives-importance-techniques-examples-methods-types-and-tools/18225

- Distributing free samples and trial packs of products

- Contests, lucky draws, sweepstakes

- Coupons for a discount on future purchases

- Stock clearance sale

- Free gifts with every purchase

- Spin a wheel or spin a fortune

- Scratch card offer

- Gifts for collection and redemption of rewards points

- Early bird offers

- Happy Hours discount during non-peak hours

- Exchange / Trade-in offers

- Money back or buy back offer

- End of Season Sale

- Thematic promotions during big events /occasions/festivals

- Seconds sale of slightly defective but usable products

- Thanksgiving Day Offers

- Cash backs or rewards

Consumer promotional schemes with instant additional gain for the consumers are most likely to give the best results. Consumer promotion tools are ideally implemented along with advertising to create mass appeal.

**Figure 9.1  Consumer Promotion Tools**

The objectives of consumer promotion can be manifold as follows:

- Induce consumers to try a new product. E.g. Giving a free trial pack

- Induce consumers to buy more, buy big, buy now, buy in advance E.g. Special reduced price for bigger pack sizes, yearly subscriptions, etc.

- Offer more value to the consumers. E.g. Giving more quantity or higher quality of the product at the existing price

- Reward consumers for frequent purchases. E.g. Giving cash backs on every purchase

- Get buyers of competing brands to migrate to marketer's brand. E.g. Exchange brand A's product, and get a price off on brand B's product

- Make consumers shift to new technology. E.g. Exchanging a VCD player for a DVD player

- Cross-promote brands/line extensions. E.g. Maggi Noodles free with Maggi Sauce

- Establish brand engagement with the consumers. E.g. Maggi Best Recipe Contest

- To retain top of the mind recall for the brand by engaging the consumers through sales promotions

- To promote new stores by incentivizing consumers to visit the store. E.g. Free products for every 100th visitor

The most common consumer promotions provide an enhanced product value, either by decreasing the price or adding more benefits to the current price. However, different promotions are used for different objectives and outcomes as follows:

## Price-Offs

Price-off is the most preferred way to sell multiple units of the products and should be advertised in advance and at the point of sale. Moreover, consumers prefer to shop more when given flat price-offs, which give instant gain and stimulate impulse buying.

## Coupons

Widely used by marketers worldwide, coupons are a great way to offer instant discounts on certain products. Coupon codes that can be redeemed against a purchase can be given to the consumer through various ways like a flyer, email, SMS, WhatsApp message, etc.

## Contests & Sweepstakes

Contests and sweepstakes help increase engagement with the brand. Contests can be based on talent, intellect, skill, and luck, whereas sweepstakes are based on luck alone. Contests and sweepstakes do not require a consumer to purchase any product and offer the potential customers an opportunity to win something. Contests can also be used to gather basic information about the consumers for communicating future promotions.

## Rewards

Rewarding the consumer for some action will benefit the marketer (e.g., suggesting the marketer's brand to a friend gives the consumer and his/her friend attractive discounts).

## Sampling

Sampling allows the consumers to experience the product for free without any purchase commitment. Free samples help consumers to test the product quality. However, this activity can be an expensive proposition as several thousand samples will have to be distributed. It can also be a logistical challenge.

## Rebates

Rebates or cash backs are given after a purchase has been made to induce repeat purchases. Nowadays, rebates are credited to the customer's app account immediately after delivery of the product.

## Premium

In premium sales promotion, an extra product is bundled in the same pack without any additional cost for the consumer.

Premiums can also be in the form of a surprise gift inside the product packaging.

## Loyalty Programs

It is a tool that rewards the customers for frequent purchases by giving them loyalty points which can be redeemed against gifts to encourage brand loyalty. Loyalty points can also be used to buy gift vouchers of other leading brands with whom the marketer has a tie-up.

## Trade-ins

Trade-ins give consumers a price mark-down if they exchange a product that they already own for buying a new or upgraded version of the same product. Trade-ins are used to fulfill the following objectives:

a. Making consumers shift from a competing brand to the marketer's brand

b. Making consumers upgrade to new technology

c. Making consumers upgrade to a better quality product

Consumer promotions should be well-planned in advance and should be thematically relevant to entice the consumers.

Some of the gifts and prizes that can be given as part of consumer promotions include the following:

- Merchandise and accessories like T-shirts, watches, bags, mouse pads, etc.

- Gift vouchers of super-markets, department stores, online shopping portals, etc.

- Coupons for restaurants, hotel stays, amusement parks, movie tickets etc.

- Merchandise with the autograph of celebrities who are brand ambassadors of the marketer's brand

- Shopping goods like mobile phones, kitchen appliances, white goods etc.

- Cars or two-wheelers for the best contest winner or lucky draw winner

Free merchandise or gifts should ideally carry the brand and marketer's logo to ensure brand recall.

## 9.1.1 Advantages of Consumer Promotion

- It helps brands maintain a consistent brand engagement with the consumers

- It increases sales volumes as intermediaries have to maintain additional inventory to meet the surge in demand due to the promotion

- It helps to gain more shelf space and visibility at the point of sale as retailers display the products prominently to create awareness for the promotional offers

- It prevents the consumers from migrating to the competitor's brand as they purchase products in advance for their future requirements as well as to avail of the offer

## 9.1.2 Challenges involved in Consumer Promotion

- Ensuring that the free merchandise, gifts, coupons, scratch cards are made available at the point of sale well in advance. Otherwise, it may lead to consumer dissatisfaction if the additional gain is not provided immediately after the purchase.

- Local statutory laws and guidelines in some regions may not allow the use of certain sales promotional activities. E.g., In some countries, any activity based on luck or chance of winning, like sweepstakes or a lucky draw, is not allowed as such activity is classified under 'Gambling.' Hence such regulations should be mandatorily followed.

- There should be an equitable distribution of gifts/prizes of all types and value across all the markets as per their sales potential. Otherwise it may lead to resentment of consumers and intermediaries in the markets which don't receive the proportionate amount of gifts or prizes.

- For any mass-scale sales promotional activity to be successful, it should be supported by mass-scale advertising to create awareness for the offer. This calls for additional advertising spending.

- Frequent consumer promotions should be avoided; otherwise, the brand will get permanently tagged as a 'Discount Brand' by the consumers.

# 9.2 Trade Promotions

Like the end consumer, the sales intermediaries also need incentives to buy more of the marketer's products. Trade promotions help the marketer to achieve this objective. Trade promotions are even more critical while doing consumer promotions. These should be implemented simultaneously with consumer promotions so that the wholesalers, retailers, agents, and other intermediaries stock up the marketer's products to meet any surge in demand while the consumer promotions are on. It also helps create increased awareness about the consumer offer and increase brand visibility at the point of sale. Some of the trade promotional activities that can be carried out are as follows (see Figure 9.2).

- Target achievement bonus for the intermediaries

- Gifts, holiday vouchers, silver or gold coins on target achievement

- Trade schemes like Buy 10 Get 1 Free for the marketer's products

- Free merchandise like T-shirts, bags, watches, etc., for the intermediaries as well as their sales staff members. This motivates them to push the products in the sales channel further

- Organizing product launch events for the intermediaries

- Incentives for the retailers to put up dealer boards of the marketer's products, give prominent window/shelf display for marketer's products, or place a product display or demonstration unit at the point of sale

- Scratch card offers for intermediaries

- Prizes for 'Best Point of Sale' display contest to enhance brand visibility

- Certificate of recognition as the 'Top Performer' or 'Best Channel Partner' for achieving sales targets

- Organizing new product launch events and press conferences at key account stores to promote new products

**Figure 9.2** **Trade Promotion Tools**

The objectives of conducting trade promotions are as follows:

- Pushing the products in the sales channel to maintain adequate inventory to minimize stock-out situations, especially when consumer promotions are being implemented

- Creating enhanced brand visibility at the point of sale, especially during a new product launch

- Regularly rewarding the intermediaries for their loyalty

- Motivating the sales team members of the intermediaries by giving them the free gifts or merchandise being distributed for consumer promotions

# Chapter Summary

◆ Sales promotions are an effective tool to increase demand in the short term as they provide instant and additional gain to the consumers as well as the intermediaries

◆ Consumer and trade promotions should ideally be implemented simultaneously for better results

◆ Consumer promotions should be planned well in advance and should be supported by mass-scale advertising for best results

# Quiz 9

1. Sales Promotion is an incentive given to the consumers to stimulate _____ purchase.

    a. long term

    b. short term

    c. medium term

    d. very long term

2. Sales Promotions should generate _____ action for a product or service.

    a. recurrent

    b. non-measurable

    c. measurable

    d. none of the above

3. What does BOGO consumer promotion offer stand for?

    a. Best One Get One

    b. Buy One Get Offer

    c. Best One Get offer

    d. Buy One Get One Free

**4. Which of the following is not a sales promotion activity?**

   a. Giving price off

   b. Giving coupons

   c. Advertising

   d. Giving a trial pack

**5. Which of the following is a consumer promotion activity?**

   a. Stock Clearance Sale

   b. Spin a Wheel

   c. Sweepstake

   d. All of the above

**6. Which of the following is not a consumer promotion activity?**

   a. Rebate

   b. Trade-in

   c. Sampling

   d. Trade scheme

**7. Which of the following is a trade promotion activity?**

   a. Spin a fortune

   b. Point of sale display contest

   c. Combo packs at reduced prices

   d. BOGO

8. **Consumer promotions should be ideally supported with _____ for maximum results.**

   a. advertising

   b. personal selling

   c. marketing

   d. all of the above

9. **Which of the following is a consumer promotion activity?**

   a. Exchange offer

   b. Money back offer

   c. Happy hours discount

   d. All of the above

10. **_____is a consumer promotion in which consumers can exchange an old product for a new one.**

    a. Rebate

    b. Trade-in

    c. Premium

    d. None of the above

| **Answers** | 1 – b | 2 – c | 3 – d | 4 – c | 5 – d |
|-------------|-------|-------|-------|-------|-------|
|             | 6 – d | 7 – b | 8 – a | 9 – d | 10 – b |

# CASE STUDY:
## Lay's Sales Promotion: 'Do me a flavor'[9]

*Lay's potato chips increased sales by using crowdsourcing to ask its fans to do them a "flavor."*

Lay's started this competition in 2012 and has seen great results. Fans can submit flavor ideas on Lay's Facebook page, and the winning flavor can win $1 million or 1% of the chip flavor's sales for that year. Lays has used crowdsourcing to encourage customers to dream up new flavors and vote for their favorites.

In this campaign, Lay's creates value by driving traffic to their Facebook page, a very relevant topic of conversation for their target millennial customers. Beyond building brand equity, this creates value by producing new chip flavors that might not exist otherwise, like Cappuccino, Wasabi Ginger, and Mango Salsa. These creative flavors have become fan favorites, driving Lay's sales up and serving new customers. In its first year, for example, the winning chip flavor, Cheesy Garlic Bread, drove an 8% sales increase for Lay's in the three months following the competition. Value is created for consumers as they have a new fun activity in brainstorming flavor ideas and feeling like they are contributing to America's favorite chip brand. Finally, this successful program sets an example for other struggling CPG brands searching for a way to connect with customers through crowdsourcing.

Lay's captures value by enjoying increased sales and positive brand equity. In 2014, Lay's received 14.4 million flavor

---

9. https://digital.hbs.edu/platform-digit/submission/lays-increases-sales-by-asking-customers-to-do-us-a-flavor/

submissions and ad recognition and purchase intent; both increased during the campaign.

Lay's has evolved the competition over the years and in 2015 took steps to turn the submissions into a two-way conversation with fans. The brand listened to customer conversations on Twitter and created funny response videos on YouTube to react to their comments. Set in a puppet show theme featuring two potatoes, the Taste Spuds, Lay's uses this medium to further engage with top influencers and extend the buzz of the competition.

Lay's has enjoyed the success of crowdsourcing in an industry that is not typically driven by its customers' creativity. Through this competition, they have incentivized customers to participate in crowdsourcing with the opportunity to win $1 million, and in return, the company has captured far more significant benefits.

## Discussion and Assignment

1. How can Lay's further innovate in the coming years to keep the contest appealing to the target audience?

2. Identify a brand in another product category that has used a similar theme for its sales promotion.

# Chapter **10**

# Sales Force Management

The sales force is the human resource of an organization that is responsible for selling its products and services. It is responsible for servicing existing customers and identifying potential customers, communicating the product details to them, persuading them to buy the products, ensuring that the products are delivered as promised, and finally collecting payment for the goods sold. Thus, the sales force is one of the most critical human resources on which the success of an organization depends. It is the sales force that interacts with the customers and brings in sales revenue for the organization. It is, thus, the face of the organization and is responsible for customer satisfaction. This chapter focuses on various aspects of sales force management which are integral to effective sales management.

Key learnings from this chapter include the reader's understanding of the following:

- What is meant by sales force management, and what are its components?

- How to recruit, train, manage, motivate, evaluate, and reward the salesforce?

- What is sales territory planning, and how to assign sales targets to the sales force?

# 10.1 Importance of Sales Force Management

Salesforce management is essential as it helps in laying out a defined sales strategy which in turn helps in streamlining the sales operations and gaining better market knowledge. (see Figure 10.1)

**Figure 10.1** Importance of Sales Force Management

- Defined Sales Strategy
- Streamlined Sales Operations
- Better Market Knowledge

# 10.2 Components of Sales Force Management

The components of sales force management are illustrated in Figure 10.2.

**Figure 10.2** | Components of Salesforce Management

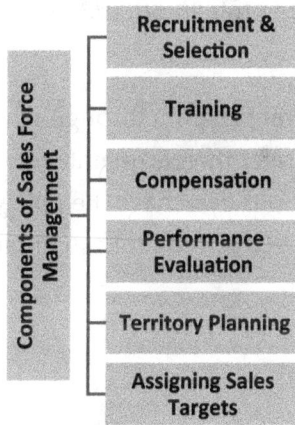

Components of Sales Force Management
- Recruitment & Selection
- Training
- Compensation
- Performance Evaluation
- Territory Planning
- Assigning Sales Targets

## 10.2.1 Salesforce recruitment and selection

While recruiting the sales force, any organization will have to define the following: -

a. Total sales force size to be recruited

b. Levels, designations, and roles for which the force has to be recruited

c. Sources of recruitment and selection criteria for the recruitment

d. Compensation to be offered to the sales force members

An organization will have to arrive at the size of its salesforce to be recruited based on the scale of its operations and the organization's internal recruitment policy. Once that has been decided, the organization can look at the following sources of recruitment:

## Internal sources

1. Existing employees who can be promoted and/or transferred for the role/location/department in which the vacancy exists

2. Employee referral program through which existing employees can refer their acquaintances for the vacancy. Some organizations even have the policy to reward their employees monetarily if their acquaintances get recruited by the organization

## External Sources

1. Recruitment advertisement in newspapers

2. Online employment portals

3. Educational institutes for fresh graduate recruits

4. Employment agencies or HR consultants

5. Poaching from other organizations

6. References from business associates

7. Job fairs for entry-level jobs

**The selection criteria should include the following parameters:**

1. Academic qualifications and achievements

2. Aptitude, communication skills, grooming

3. Experience in relevant product category or industry

4. Size of territory and team managed in the past

5. Volume and value of sales handled

6. Team management and leadership skills

7. Network and contacts developed in the industry

8. Knowledge about statutory regulations

9. Understanding of market dynamics

10. Any other professional achievements

**The selection process should ideally be as follows:**

1. Sourcing candidate profiles through internal and external sources

2. Selection tests (Aptitude/Personality/Psychometric/Case Study)

3. Screening of profiles by Human Resource (HR) department

4. Personal interview with HR personnel

5. Personal interview with reporting superior

6. Medical check-up for fitness certificate

7. Personal interview with the final decision-making authority

8. Letters of recommendation from references mentioned by the candidates

9. Finalizing the compensation or salary

10. Employment offer and appointment letter on joining

## 10.2.2 Salesforce training

Once the employees join the organization, they should be given training using one or more of the following methods:

1. Product information through product catalog/website

2. Simulated techniques by using computer software to simulate a real-world scenario

3. Role plays to replicate a live situation in the classroom

4. Field visit with sales team member/superior

5. Training on the sales documentation process

6. Soft skills and personality development workshops

7. Training at designated training centers of the organization

8. Any other relevant method

## 10.2.3 Salesforce compensation

The salesforce has to be compensated and motivated through one or more of the following ways:

### Monetary compensation

1. Joining bonus

2. Basic salary

3. House Rent Allowance (HRA)

4. Dearness Allowance (DA)

5. Traveling Allowance

6. Target-based incentive

7. Performance and promotion-based salary increase

8. Loyalty bonus

9. Fuel allowance

10. Reimbursement of medical expenses

11. Provident Fund

12. Gratuity

13. Any other

## Non-monetary compensation

1. Promotion to a higher level

2. Target-based incentives in kind, e.g., paid vacations, gifts

3. Car and chauffeur

4. Company-owned accommodation

5. Company-sponsored training workshops or further education

6. Job enrichment to give higher order of responsibility

7. ESOPs (Equity Stock Ownership Plan), i.e., giving equity shares of the company

8. Recognition through certificates, trophies, or medals

9. Motivation from superiors for work accomplishment

## 10.2.4 Evaluating sales force performance

The performance of the sales force should be evaluated on the following parameters:

### Quantitative parameters

- Sales target achievement (based on volume, value, or profitability)

- Average on-field or off-field customers/prospects attended

- Number of new customer accounts developed

- Effective sales territory management

- Level of product knowledge and awareness

### Qualitative parameters

- Relationship management with sales intermediaries

- Conflict management skills

- Negotiation skills

- Effective coordination with other sales/marketing team members

## 10.2.5 Sales territory planning

A sales territory is a marked market space allocated to each salesperson and consists of existing customers and prospects.

## Advantages of mapping sales territories

1. Aids in salesforce planning by allocating territory to each salesperson

2. Maintaining and increasing market penetration and coverage

3. Controlling sales expenses by effectively planning the route/ journey plan of each salesperson

4. Better evaluation of sales force performance as per territory assigned to each salesperson

The topography of a region influences a sales territory route plan. Some of the route plans are as follows:

## Straight Line Route Plan

This plan is ideal for regions where the region's development is linear from the base location. (See Figure 10.3)

**Figure 10.3** **Straight Line Route Plan**

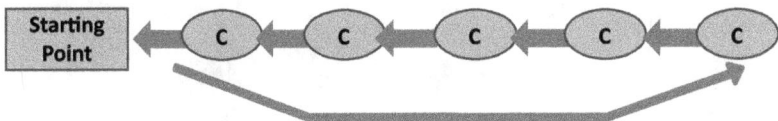

C = Customer

**Copyright-** Houghton Mifflin Harcourt Publishing Company.

## Circular Route Plan

This plan is ideal for regions where the region's development is in a circular pattern with many areas around the periphery of the base location. (see Figure 10.4)

**Figure 10.4** | **Circular Route Plan**

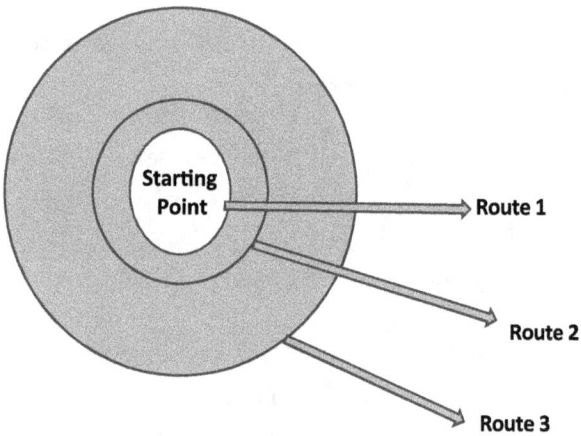

**Copyright-** Houghton Mifflin Harcourt Publishing Company.

## Clover Leaf Route Plan

This plan is ideal for regions where the region's development is in a cloverleaf pattern from the base location. (see Figure 10.5)

**Figure 10.5** Clover Leaf Route Plan

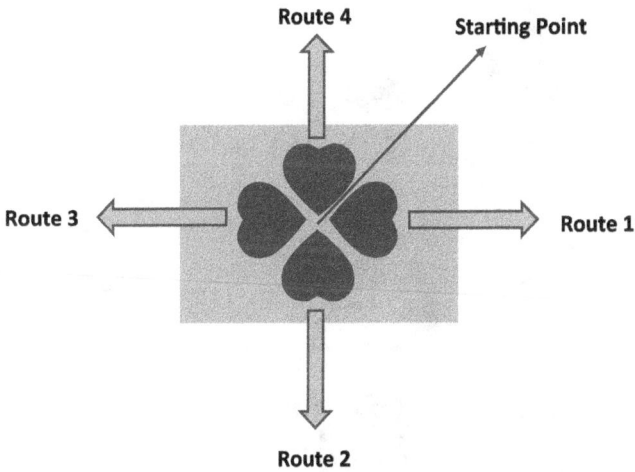

**Copyright-** Houghton Mifflin Harcourt Publishing Company.

## Hopscotch Route Plan

This plan is ideal for regions where the region's development is on all sides of the base location and in a hopscotch pattern. (see Figure 10.6)

**Figure 10.6** **Hopscotch Route Plan**

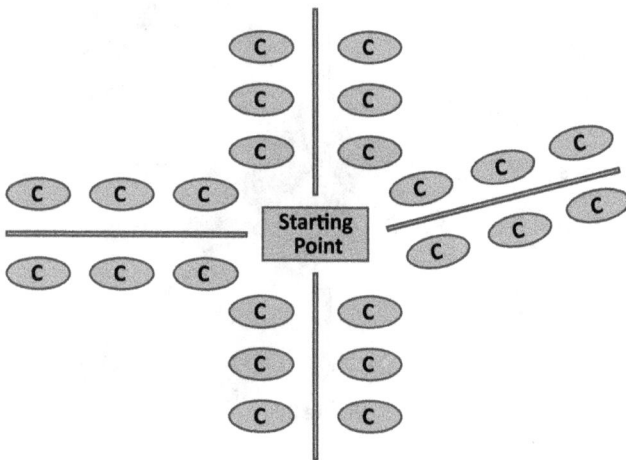

C = Customer

Copyright- Houghton Mifflin Harcourt Publishing Company.

## Use of IT in Sales Management

- To map out the most effective route plan, IT software is available in the market, which can help devise multiple permutations and combinations of route plans for optimal territory planning.

- Sales automation software can be used to automate repetitive tasks such as follow-up with customers for renewal of their subscription, re-ordering of products bought earlier, reminders for payment on the due date.

## 10.2.6 Assigning sales targets

Sales targets for the salesforce can be assigned in any one of the following ways:

### Territory wise targets

- Each salesperson is assigned one or more geographical territories to manage

- Each territory has a different number of customers and prospects with varying sales potential

- The sales target for each salesperson is thus calculated based on the total potential of the respective territories

### Fixed number of customers

- Each salesperson handles a fixed number of customers and prospect accounts

- Each salesperson has a mix of customers and prospects with varying sales potential

- The sales target for each salesperson is decided based on the total potential of all the accounts

### Category wise customer allocation

- Customers are classified as per their sales potential into various categories, e.g., A, B, C Accounts

- Each salesperson is allocated one category of customers to handle

- The sales target of each salesperson will vary depending upon the sales potential of each category of customers

# 10.3 Benefits of Sales Force Management

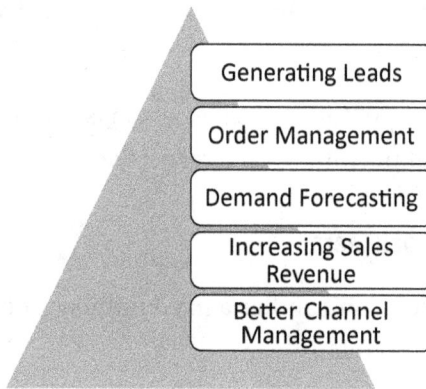

The benefits of sales force management are illustrated in Figure 10.7.

**Figure 10.7** **Benefits of Sales Force Management**

Generating Leads

Order Management

Demand Forecasting

Increasing Sales Revenue

Better Channel Management

# Chapter Summary

◆ Salesforce management involves multiple activities like salesforce selection, training, evaluation, and rewarding

◆ Salesforce management helps to establish, maintain and improve the standards of sales effectiveness in an organization

◆ Sales automation software can also be used to automate specific repetitive processes to increase sales effectiveness and reduce costs of sales force management

# Quiz 10

1. **Salesforce management involves the following _____.**

   a. recruitment

   b. training

   c. evaluation

   d. all of the above

2. **Salesforce management helps in _____.**

   a. better sales operations

   b. defined sales strategy

   c. new product launch

   d. options A & B

3. **Advertising in news-papers for vacancies is _____ source of recruitment.**

   a. internal

   b. external

   c. reference

   d. all of the above

4. **Which of the following employment methods is ideal for recruitment of salesforce at entry-level?**

   a. References from a business associate

   b. Campus hiring

   c. Poaching from other organizations

   d. All of the above

5. **Which of the following is an internal source of recruitment?**

   a. Promotion of existing employee

   b. Employee referral program

   c. Transfer of existing employee

   d. All of the above

6. **Which of the following is not an external source of recruitment?**

   a. Educational institutes

   b. Job Fairs

   c. Promoting an existing employee

   d. Online job portals

7. **The selection process for salesforce recruitment should include which of the following?**

   a. Aptitude test

   b. Personal interview

   c. Medical fitness check

   d. All of the above

**8. Which of the following is a method of salesforce training?**

    a. On the field-training

    b. Simulated training

    c. Role play

    d. All of the above

**9. Which of the following is compensation in kind?**

    a. Traveling allowance

    b. Dearness allowance

    c. Loyalty bonus

    d. Paid Vacation

**10. Which of the following is a non-monetary compensation?**

    a. Reimbursement of fuel expenses

    b. Provident Fund

    c. Job enrichment

    d. None of the above

| **Answers** | 1 – d | 2 – d | 3 – b | 4 – b | 5 – d |
|---|---|---|---|---|---|
| | 6 – c | 7 – d | 8 – d | 9 – d | 10 – c |

# CASE STUDY:
# SalesForce Performance Evaluation

A company has to disburse a yearly bonus to its salesforce. For that, it has to evaluate the relative performance of each salesperson based on their individual sales achievement data. (See Table 10. 1)

| Table 10.1 | Sales achievement data for each salesperson |

| Sales person | Total order value | Total market potential | Calls per week | No. of orders | Avg. order value |
|---|---|---|---|---|---|
| A | 1,00,000 | 4,00,000 | 40 | 20 | 5,000 |
| B | 90,000 | 9,00,000 | 90 | 90 | 1,000 |
| C | 2,00,000 | 5,00,000 | 50 | 20 | 10,000 |
| D | 3,20,000 | 8,50,000 | 200 | 160 | 2,000 |

The company has decided to evaluate the performance of each salesperson as follows:

a. Percentage of market potential converted into orders – higher the percentage, higher the score

b. Average order value per order- higher the value, higher the score

c. Calls made to order conversion ratio – higher the ratio higher the score

The total score is then calculated for each salesperson as illustrated in Table 10.2. The one who scores the highest is the best performer and should get the highest bonus amount.

| Table 10.2 | Calculation of total score for each salesperson |
| --- | --- |

| Sales person | Market potential converted into orders | Score (out of 10) | Avg. order value | Score (out of 10) | calls to order conversion ratio | Score (out of 10) | Total Score | Rank |
| --- | --- | --- | --- | --- | --- | --- | --- | --- |
| A | 25% | 2.5 | 5000 | 5 | 50% | 5 | 12.5 | 3rd |
| B | 10% | 1 | 1000 | 1 | 100% | 10 | 12 | 4th |
| C | 40% | 4 | 10000 | 10 | 40% | 4 | 18 | 1st |
| D | 38% | 3.8 | 2000 | 2 | 80% | 8 | 13.8 | 2nd |

As per Table 10.2, salesperson C is the best performer and should get the highest bonus amount.

# Class Assignment

## SalesForce Performance Evaluation

Table 10.3 lists the sales performances data of four salespersons. Which salesperson has performed the best?

**Table 10.3**    **Sales performance data of salespersons**

| Sales person | Total order value | Total market potential | Calls per week | No. of orders | Avg. order value |
|---|---|---|---|---|---|
| A | 2,00,000 | 4,00,000 | 50 | 20 | 10,000 |
| B | 1,80,000 | 9,00,000 | 100 | 90 | 2,000 |
| C | 4,00,000 | 5,00,000 | 50 | 50 | 8,000 |
| D | 4,25,000 | 8,50,000 | 170 | 85 | 5,000 |

## Solution

Salesperson C has performed the best as per evaluation illustrated in Table 10.4.

**Table 10.4**    **Sales performance evaluation of each sales person**

| Sales person | Market potential to order ratio | Score (out of 10) | Avg. order value | Score (out of 10) | calls to order conversion ratio | Score (out of 10) | Total Score | Rank |
|---|---|---|---|---|---|---|---|---|
| A | 50% | 5 | 10,000 | 10 | 40% | 4 | 19 | 2nd |
| B | 20% | 2 | 2,000 | 2 | 90% | 9 | 13 | 3rd |
| C | 80% | 8 | 8,000 | 8 | 100% | 10 | 26 | 1st |
| D | 50% | 5 | 2,000 | 2 | 50% | 5 | 12 | 4th |

*This page is intentionally left blank*

# Chapter **11**

# Sales Management Post-Pandemic

Irrespective of the company's size, the industry it operates in, the nature of its competition, or consumer demand, an organization's sales team remains under stress during any pandemic. Customer relationship management changes its dimensions as companies reorganize their sales structures and processes during and after the pandemic. This puts additional pressure on the sales team to align with the new normal. Hence, evaluating the post-pandemic sales strategies is a must as companies recover from a forced economic recession.

The key learnings from this chapter include the reader's understanding of the following:

- How does a pandemic influence the sales management landscape?

- What should organizations do to adapt to the pandemic-induced changes in consumer behavior?

> • What changes in the sales management strategies are needed in a post-pandemic business environment?

The post-pandemic recovery conditions vary from market to market as demand increases across industries. Though offline meetings are possible, a hybrid work schedule continues till the pandemic subsides considerably. At the same time, the focus of sales efforts shifts from survival mode to growth and recovery mode. Eventually, the new normal also gets diluted and turns 'back to normal' as people start attending offices and face-to-face meetings become possible. Given these circumstances, the following are some of the post-pandemic sales strategies that may need to be pursued once things are back to normal:

### Review the product portfolio

The pandemic may have changed the companies' product mix to suit the pandemic-induced change in consumers' buying preferences. Hence, it becomes essential to relook at the product portfolio to identify any changes that may be needed concerning the same. Customers may have discontinued consuming certain products, brands, or SKUs during the pandemic. Thus, it is necessary to review the product mix to suit the post-pandemic buying behavior of consumers, as they are likely to be more selective while spending money.

## Focus on retaining existing customers

In a B2B context, reaching out to potential customers proves to be more challenging in a pandemic. The accessibility to decision-makers in an organization reduces considerably during the pandemic as they might not be attending office. Hence, retaining the existing customer base is of prime importance than looking for new ones.

## Adapt to changing sales fulfillment channels

In a B2C context, following a multi-channel demand fulfillment strategy may become necessary once the pandemic ends. Focusing more on an omni-channel strategy, which is skewed towards emerging sales channels, may help streamline sales operations faster. However, before arriving at any conclusions regarding channel preferences of the consumers post-pandemic, thorough research is required to understand trends in consumer behavior.

## Re-segment your markets

Market segments that a marketer catered to before the pandemic may no longer be profitable enough to justify the resources allocated to them. Identify the market segments which require more face-to-face interactions with the decision makers vis-a-vis segments that can be on a 'self-service' mode of purchasing your products. Accordingly, allocate resources for optimum productivity. Face-to-face sales pitches should be preferred for bigger deals which may also require a customized approach for providing solutions to the complex needs of the customers.

## Leverage digitization and sales-automation tools

Sales digitization and automation gain importance during any situation, which warrants that people stay at home. Customers and marketers across industries align themselves to digitization tools due to the pandemic. At the same time, various sales tools are emerging that can help sales teams to optimize sales processes and enhance effectiveness tremendously. For some organizations, the pandemic may instead help them precipitate the shift to further digitization and automation to increase productivity and decrease the cost of operations. The changes that many people imagined would take years have taken place in a few weeks.

# Chapter Summary

◆ A pandemic changes the way sales teams operate in a post-pandemic business environment. Some of these changes are short-term and temporary, whereas some are permanent with long-term implications

◆ Marketers and salespersons will have to stay relevant to the post-pandemic requirements of their customers and prospects by following the best practices adopted by their counterparts

◆ Organizations which show resilience and flexibility in their sales management approach will be able to face the pandemic in an effective manner

*This page is intentionally left blank*

# Glossary

**Advertising:** Communicating the availability and features of a product to the consumers and sales channel intermediaries.

**Brand Extension:** Launching a new product using an existing brand name.

**Business to Consumer (B2C):** Selling products to an individual consumer by a marketer through a chain of intermediaries.

**Business to Business (B2B):** Selling of products by a marketer to organizations for their internal consumption.

**Business to Business (B2G):** Selling of products by a marketer to government organizations for their internal consumption.

**Channel Conflict:** Situation of discord or disagreement between members or intermediaries of a sales channel.

**Channel Width:** Number of intermediaries in the sales channel.

**Channel Partner or Sales Intermediary:** Distributor, wholesaler, retailer or agent, who sells the marketer's products.

**Concept Selling:** Selling an idea rather than a product that fulfills the current, future, and aspirational needs of the consumers.

**Consumer:** An individual or an organization who buys products or services available in the marketplace to satisfy their needs.

**Consumer Promotions:** Sales promotion tools to induce or incentivize the consumer to buy a marketer's products by offering additional gratification.

**Cross-Selling:** Selling a product that is complementary or supplementary to the product that consumers intend to buy.

**Direct to Consumer (D2C):** Selling products directly to the consumers without involving any intermediaries.

**Diversification:** Launching a new product in a new product category and with a different brand name.

**Form Utility:** Value derived by providing a product in a ready-to-consume state to the consumers.

**Inventory:** Quantity of any product available in a ready-to-sell condition at any given point in time.

**Key Account:** Customer who buys products in large volumes directly from a marketer rather than through intermediaries.

**Key Account Management:** Effectively managing the Key Accounts to achieve the sales objectives of the marketer.

**Line Extension:** The strategy of launching multiple variants of an existing brand within the existing product category.

**Marketer:** Any organization that manufactures goods or provides services and sells them to the consumers either directly or through sales intermediaries.

**Marketing:** Identifying unfulfilled needs or wants of the consumers and satisfying the same through a product offering.

**Marketing Concept:** An approach which states that profits can be earned by satisfying consumers' needs rather than by just selling existing products manufactured in a factory.

**Multi-Brand Strategy:** The strategy of having multiple brands in the same product category.

**Omni Channel:** Offering the consumers an option to choose how to purchase, collect or return products as per their convenience through offline or online mode.

**Product:** Market offering in terms of tangible good or intangible service that satisfies a consumer's need or want.

**Place Utility:** Value derived by making a product available as close as possible to the consumers.

**Possession Utility:** Value derived by transferring the possession of the product to the consumers.

**Product & Brand Mix:** Portfolio of products and brands of a marketer.

**Push Sales:** Selling of products primarily through sales efforts directed towards the channel intermediaries.

**Pull Sales:** Selling of products primarily through advertising efforts directed towards the end consumers.

**Sales:** A transaction that involves transfer of possession and ownership of tangible goods from the seller to the buyer and/or performance of a particular set of activities (services) by the seller for the benefit of the buyer, in return for a consideration from the buyer.

**Sales Channel:** Chain of intermediaries through which a marketer sells its product or services.

**Sales Management:** Planning and executing all tasks concerned with selling, selling techniques, sales force management, and distribution of goods and services.

**Sales Force Management:** Analysis, planning, implementation, and control of sales force activities.

**Sales Territory Planning:** Planning the journey or route plan of the sales force to cover the market area effectively.

**Selling Concept:** An approach which states that profits can be earned by selling huge volumes of existing products manufactured in a factory.

**Stock Keeping Unit (SKU):** A distinct unit of a product based on brand name, variant, pack size, or any other attribute.

**Street Price:** The retail price of products.

**T**rade Promotions: Sales promotion tools that incentivize the sales channel intermediaries to buy more of the marketer's products.

**Time Utility:** Value derived by making a product available to the consumers as fast as possible.

**U**p-selling: Selling a premium or an upgraded version of a product.

**V**alue: A bundle of benefits that a consumer seeks from using a product or a service.

**Value-added selling:** Offering more value to the consumers than the value offered by the competitors without making them spend additional money on the products they buy.

**Variant:** A distinct unit of a product or a brand with distinguishable attribute like color, shape, size, taste, flavor, fragrance, etc.

# Notes